ANCIENT CYPRUS

HEAD IN LIMESTONE OF THE FOURTH CENTURY, B.C.
FROM ARSOS
(*Nicosia Museum*)

ANCIENT CYPRUS
Its Art and Archaeology

by
STANLEY CASSON
M.A., F.S.A., Hon. A.R.I.B.A.

READER IN CLASSICAL ARCHAEOLOGY IN THE UNIVERSITY
OF OXFORD, FELLOW OF NEW COLLEGE ; MEMBER OF
THE GERMAN ARCHAEOLOGICAL INSTITUTE, AND
CORRESPONDING MEMBER OF THE BULGARIAN
ARCHAEOLOGICAL INSTITUTE

WITH 16 PLATES
AND A MAP

GREENWOOD PRESS, PUBLISHERS
WESTPORT, CONNECTICUT

Reprinted from an original copy in the collections
of the Yale University Library

Originally published in 1937 by
Methuen & Co., Ltd., London

First Greenwood Reprinting 1970

Library of Congress Catalogue Card Number 70- 95086

SBN 8371-3080-8

Printed in the United States of America

PREFACE

CYPRUS is the only British possession which serves to illustrate the history and activities of the Greeks. Its contributions to our knowledge of Greek art and history are numerous and important. It has long had attached to it the label of 'Oriental' without any attempt being made to see how far that description referred to superficial elements in its life. I prefer to see the history and art of the Cypriots as those of Oriental Greeks rather than of Hellenized Orientals. For in many respects Cyprus retained more qualities which are ancient Greek, or perhaps Achaean, than any area of the Greek world. The Orient bore upon it at times with overwhelming force, but the Greek element always seemed to emerge in the end.

Cyprus itself is a paradise of natural beauty and contains at the same time many masterpieces of medieval Gothic and Byzantine art. Admiration for these all too often diverts attention from its supremely interesting history in the Mycenaean period as well as from its occasional periods of artistic activity in the Bronze Age and in Classical times. Cyprus is by no means a desert in which occasional oases of artistic creation are slowly killed by an arid tradition. There is much originality in its artistic outlook and much great achievement. Our judgements of Cypriot ability have been too long overclouded by the unjustified assumption that everything Cypriot is mediocre.

Cyprus preserved much that was ancient and forgotten in the Greek world. Among other things Cyprus retained the kingship (which as far as I can see

v

had no Oriental affinities) and also a mode of writing inherited from Minoan times. It was the only place in the Greek world where Greek was written in a medium other than the Greek alphabet. To this subject I have paid particular attention in this book, concentrating mainly on the Bronze Age Cypriot script which has never hitherto been fully examined.

No study of Cyprus could be undertaken without reference to the pioneer work of Professor J. L. Myres. He can be looked upon as the founder of Cypriot archaeology and its most learned exponent. To him is largely due the work which made it possible for Cyprus to have a well-organized service of archaeology. His Catalogue of the Cyprus Museum and of the Cesnola Collection in New York still remain our principal repositories for information of Cypriot antiquities. I acknowledge here unhesitatingly my debt to his work. He was the first to bring order into chaos and the first to explain the innumerable problems of Cypriot archaeology. What he did has not been superseded, least of all by this book.

Finally, I must acknowledge the very great help afforded me by Mr. Dikaios, Curator of the Nicosia Museum, both in the matter of information and of illustrations. To Professor Myres also I am deeply indebted for reading my proofs and making many suggestions and corrections.

So much has been done in the last quarter of a century to add to our knowledge of Cyprus that I feel that a general reconsideration of the principal problems is not unwanted.

S. C.

NEW COLLEGE,
OXFORD

CONTENTS

vii

ILLUSTRATIONS

I HAVE to acknowledge permission to use the following :

Plates II, VII, IX, and X, to Mr. O. G. S. Crawford.

Plates I, III, V, XIII, 1 and XV, 1 and 2, to Mr. P. Dikaios, Curator of the Nicosia Museum.

Plate VI to the Trustees of the Metropolitan Museum, New York.

Plates IV and VIII to the Trustees of the British Museum.

Plates XIII, 2, and XIV to the Swedish Mission and Professor Gjerstad.

S. C.

ABBREVIATIONS

B.M. = British Museum.
C.A.R. = Cyprus Annual Report.
C.V.A. = Corpus Vasorum Antiquorum.
J.H.S. = Journal of Hellenic Studies.
J.R.A.I. and *J.A.I.* = Journal of the Royal Anthropological Institute.
P. of M. = *The Palace of Minos*, by Sir Arthur Evans.
P.-W. Pauly-Wissowa.
S.C.E. = Swedish Cyprus Expedition publications.

CHAPTER I

INTRODUCTORY

WE speak often and lightly of what we call 'insular characteristics' without always clearly understanding what we mean by this term. For some islands are, paradoxically enough, more insular than others. In our own seas it is obvious enough that the Isle of Wight is less insular than the Isle of Man and that the Scilly Islands have less mainland influences than the Channel Islands. So too in the Mediterranean the culture of Crete is more insular and isolated and peculiar to itself than the culture, say, of Samos or Lemnos or Lesbos. The culture of Rhodes at no period of time exhibits characteristics which are predominantly Rhodian. On the other hand Cyprus, like Crete, throughout its history stands, to a large extent, aloof from mainland influences even though it adopts many of them. In the whole of Cypriot history and prehistory there is always perceptible an undercurrent of influence which, for good or bad, remains Cypriot. Nothing that Cyprus absorbed from outside remained unaffected in the long run by Cypriot influences; indeed it would be incorrect to say that Cyprus absorbed anything; she rather adopted and then transformed. For it was inevitable that the island would fall under the influence of the peoples of

Asia Minor on the north, of Syria and Palestine on
the east and of Egypt on the south. But it was by
no means inevitable that she would fall under any influence from the west, partly because of the fact that
Rhodes stood as a buffer between Cyprus and Greece
and partly because at Rhodes trade routes diverged
into the Aegean, in various directions; thus traders
from the east no longer followed a main stream of
traffic once they had reached Rhodes, while traders
travelling eastwards were not necessarily tempted to
go farther than Rhodes, which to a large extent acted
as a clearing station for trade in both directions.

The history and prehistory of Cyprus is thus more
deeply involved with the neighbouring mainlands
than with the Aegean, except at one or two periods
when Aegean forces, aiming farther eastwards than
Cyprus, inevitably found themselves using the island
for their purposes. But in each case their goal was
not Cyprus itself, but rather the mainland regions to
which it was a convenient stepping-stone for maritime
peoples. Cyprus was thus never a final goal of any
external ambition and in consequence managed to
preserve her insular qualities in a way which has
always been a surprise and to some extent a puzzle to
students of history, archaeology and art.

Crete, by contrast, was the goal of mainland destruc-
tive forces and her prehistoric culture was rooted up
and destroyed by envious rivals, once in 1400 B.C.
and once again during the Dorian invasion soon after
1100 B.C. Thus the Cretans were unable to retain
much of their insular customs and characteristics.
Classical Crete differs only a little from any other

part of Classical Greece, but Classical Cyprus is unlike any other place in the Classical Hellenic world. The cultural development of Crete had been broken twice ; that of Cyprus was never broken, for no expedition and no invasion set out with the main object of destroying Cypriot civilization. Thus we find that in Cyprus there are far more survivals from one period into another, survivals from the Bronze Age to the classical period, survivals of Mycenaean characteristics into the Hellenic Age, survivals from the pre-Mycenaean Age into the Mycenaean, survivals from the Bronze Age down to to-day, survivals of language and stock and racial type from age to age. There are, indeed, few places in the world where so many inheritances from a very remote past still persist.

This habit of survival which so deeply influenced everything in the island at all periods, and which was an unrecognized undercurrent to all Cypriot modes of life, is responsible for that peculiar mode in art, which is universally recognized at almost all periods, and which is so marked as to stamp a Cypriot-made work of art almost at once as Cypriot to the expert, often even to the novice. It is equally responsible for the course which many events of Cypriot history inevitably took ; and it may be no less responsible for the earliest manner of literature associated with Cyprus. The Classical Greeks recognized it quickly enough and gave it the title of[1] *Κύπριος χαρακτήρ*, a title which had few parallels in ancient *obiter dicta*.[2]

[1] *Supplices*, 282.
[2] Pausanias (v, 25. 12) identifies also an Aeginetan style (*τέχνη Αἰγίναια*) and an Attic (*ἐργαστήριον Ἀττικόν*).

To recognize Cypriot survivals and the *Κύπριος χαρακτήρ* to-day in modified form one has to look rather at the odd and strange survivals from Byzantine religious forms and practices rather than to older strata. Certainly in Cyprus there is much that survives of the old Orthodox habits that are dead elsewhere except in Athos, and the persistence and power of Cypriot saints is one of the most remarkable features of modern life in the island. But, side by side with Byzantine survivals, one sees here and there practices, habits and tangible objects which all go back to immemorial antiquity. Most astonishing to the traveller in Cyprus is to see in every village and town the huge globular water-pots of heavy dark-red fabric, long-necked, gourd-shaped and devoid of base-rings, carried on the shoulder like immense pumpkins, placed on the ground always leaning against the wall to avoid rolling over, and often stacked in square wooden frames to prevent the same calamity. In days when every other Greek region employs water jars which either stand freely on their bases or else (as in Attica) have pointed ends which firmly grip the ground, some particular origin must be sought for these modern vessels. The source is not hard to find, for a comparison with the thousands of extant vessels of the Early and Middle Bronze Age show an identical form, and even size, fabric and colour. The similarity may, of course, be due to pure chance,[1] but it deserves more serious

---

[1] We must not overlook the influence which the continuous and repeated discovery of Bronze Age vessels in tombs by looting peasants may have had. I am unable to trace the history of the modern vessel and its type, and it may be that before the nine-

mention than it has hitherto received. It may also be possibly due to the same causes producing the same effects. Gourds are still a widespread and popular vessel in use among Cypriot peasants and the potter to-day, as in the Bronze Age, may have taken his cue from them. Even so, this natural conservatism in the face of the inventions of surrounding peoples may itself serve as proof of the persistence of habits, even if we reject the actual pottery as a survival of shape, fabric and general type. The gourd is equally in use in other Greek regions, but it does not equally influence the potter. That the Cypriot potter should continue to be so influenced is in itself of the nature of a survival.[1]

Another noteworthy and, I think, clear survival, that does not belong to the field of conjecture and fantasy is the modern Cypriot mud brick. There is nothing in the habit of making mud bricks that belongs to the realm of survival. They are made all over the Mediterranean as being the cheapest medium of building and one of the most convenient, and have been so made for thousands of years. But the modern Cypriot brick differs completely from those made in Greece

teenth century, when tomb-looting was at its height, the peasant employed a different type of vessel. No history of modern Cypriot pottery has yet been attempted.

[1] Professor J. L. Myres has remarked that ' the modern Cypriot, with characteristic conservatism, still prefers gourds for household bottles and ladles, and still incises geometrical ornaments and concentric circles upon them '. The word ' still ' when applied to the habit of making designs presupposes too much. Circles as design are so elementary a form of ornament that they can hardly be considered to have survival-value even in so conservative a region. (Myres, *Catalogue of the Cyprus Museum*, p. 16.)

2

proper and other Aegean regions.   It is thin and tile-
shaped, rather like a turf block of English peat.   The
recent excavations at Vouni Palace (see below, p. 162)
has revealed that the walls are in many places composed of mud bricks, now more hardened and consoli-
dated than when first in place.   These bricks are of the
same shape and almost of the same dimensions as the
modern example.   This comparison is not fortuitous.

Other survivals have been noted.   Some may be
due to coincidence, some may be hazardous guesses,
but all deserve mention.   Bronze scrapers are found
in various Cypriot sites : they correspond exactly in
shape with those used to-day by Cypriot women for
scraping the dough off troughs when making bread
in the ordinary way.[1]   A pair of silver loom-rings
from Poli correspond to a type of loom-ring still in use
in Cyprus.[2]   The modern three legged incense-burner
which can be bought in any village shop in Cyprus
and the small clay figures used for dedication in
churches are made by a ' mud pie ' technique which
recalls Bronze Age incense-burners and votive figures.
There are no parallels for either elsewhere in Greek
lands except in Crete, where a roughly similar incense-
burner is made.   Other and more speculative survivals
can be suggested,[3] but none are so impressive as the
pottery and the brick fashions.

[1] Myres, op. cit., p. 53.   Eight examples are in the Museum
from various sites.

[2] Op. cit., p. 138, nos. 4801–3.

[3] Cesnola (*Cyprus*, p. 180), makes a comparison between the
cloth cap worn by Greek priests as ' undress uniform ' and the
hats worn by the sculptured figures from Golgoi.

One remarkable survival—at least such I suppose it to be, though its verification can only be made by an archaeological examination—is to be found in a strange underground Turkish shrine called Kirklar,[1] a mile south of the village of Tymbou in the Mesaoria. It is known to the Greeks as Aghia Saranda. In fact, it is an underground building consisting of three aisles cut out of the rock and intercommunicating. Steps lead down to each aisle and at the end is what looks like a fountain house of the type of Peirene, though there is no water now. Round the sides are what appear to be a number of interments, covered with the sacred green silk of Islam and crowned with turban stones. These I take to be intrusive and later. The whole is so thoroughly whitewashed in the Turkish manner that one cannot see the nature of the walls. But the building has all the appearance of having been cut out of the rock. It is a sinister and impressive place and the Turkish *hodja* in charge had no kind of explanation to give of it, nor had he any legend or alleged history to record which belonged to it. It was merely the shrine of the 'Holy Forty' as its names imply, but of what Forty he had no idea. Religious susceptibilities make it impossible to clear the building, as its obvious antiquity deserves should be done. Until then we can only guess. But the place will prove to be either a Cypriot tomb or a water-fountain house of the classical age. Curiously enough, the multifarious writers who have wandered through Cyprus and recorded their wanderings in print have never even mentioned this strange place until recently.[2]

[1] Gunnis, *Historic Cyprus*, 1936, p. 453. [2] Gunnis, loc. cit.

Its proximity to the capital makes this the more remarkable, since travellers in Cyprus have overlooked
little within comfortable distance of the best hotels.

The history of archaeological research in the island
is a strange and sad history. It begins, for all practical
purposes, with the enterprises, better perhaps described
as depredations, of General Cesnola. This interesting
and vivid personality, a colonel in the American War
of Independence, reached Cyprus in 1865 appointed
by Abraham Lincoln as American consul. He has left
us a plain statement of his archaeological activities in
the ensuing years under the rule of the Turks.[1] His
account is frank and illuminating, but much more
than he tells can be gathered by reading between the
lines. It was written to dispel the belief prevalent,
as soon as news of his discoveries leaked out, that his
methods were not strictly orthodox. ' Several distinguished scholars,' he tells us, ' had expressed their
fears as to whether my excavations had been conducted
in a systematic manner,' and he adds ' that they were
perhaps not conducted in all their details according to
the usual manner adopted and advocated by most
archaeologists, I am unwilling to dispute.' In effect
General Cesnola justifiably acquired the reputation
of being the most consistent and thorough looter of
antiquities of the later nineteenth century. Nevertheless his book on Cyprus shows great knowledge, a
capacity for apt reference to recorded history and an
ingenuous appreciation of the works of art that he
discovered. The habit, which soon became a fashion,
in the next generation to make him out to be an arch-

[1] *Cyprus : its ancient cities, tombs and temples*, 1877.

robber whose ignorance and greed destroyed a vast bulk of valuable information and filled up the well of knowledge with a deposit of rubbish, is certainly not borne out by his book and by the bulk of his publications. For he acquired a considerable learning, was capable of shrewd stylistic comparisons and sound classifications, and put his material—no matter how it was accumulated—into a shape which has made the bulk of it easily accessible to subsequent study. His main collection was not dispersed, but purchased by the Metropolitan Museum, New York, the director of which he became at the same time. For Cypriot archaeology this collection will always remain the principal basis of future study.

Criticisms of Cesnola and the disputes that raged about his methods and his finds would be of greater historical value had those who came after Cesnola started at once to improve on his methods. He at least sedulously saved antiquities from destruction, and preserved them for subsequent workers. His methods were unscientific to the last degree and his own account of how he made some of his investigations [1] freezes the marrow of the present generation of scientific excavators. But he was little worse than most of the professionals of his day. Etruscan tombs had in the fifties been looted on a contract and commercial basis. Sites in England of prehistoric Roman and Saxon dates had been no less ruthlessly torn up. It was the personality of Cesnola rather than his methods that gave offence and his personality is revealed with a charming naïveté in his books.

[1] Op. cit., pp. 118–24. Excavation by proxy.

The story of Cypriot research after Cesnola has no bright spots. The list of excavations made in the island in the first few years of British rule, which are recorded by Professor Myres, make gloomy reading, while the condition of archaeological administration, museum work and preservation is a long record of decay and destruction by neglect. One is almost driven to the conclusion that the immediate successors of Cesnola in the island did as much destruction of antiquities as Cesnola did in the way of preservation. Professor Myres, who was one of the few scholars to attempt to undertake a radical reform of the state of affairs, tells us that [1] despite the law of antiquities which gave the government a third part of the produce of all excavations, the antiquities represented by this share were allowed to perish from neglect or get lost by carelessness. Many of the antiquities ' lay for years outside the Commissioner's office in Nicosia exposed to all kinds of ill-usage'. Some ' suffered serious damage'. The Museum, founded in 1883, was maintained by private subscriptions ' which soon failed to be sufficient'. Antiquities were damaged in transit for exhibition at London, tomb-groups were dispersed and ' even in the Museum the condition of the collection was deplorable'. After the catalogue was completed a number of Attic vases was ' discovered in the wardrobe of the caretaker's wife'. ' A large part of the Government collection', concluded Professor Myres, ' has lost almost all scientific value.' Yet between 1880 and 1894 when Professor Myres wrote the first catalogue of the Museum, scholars of

[1] *Catalogue of the Cyprus Museum*, p. vii.

great distinction had travelled the length and breadth
of the island, excavated, and worked in the Museum.
None of them had succeeded in stimulating in the
authorities any appreciation of the antiquities of the
island, though their combined influence might have
done much.

The record of excavations between 1880 and 1894
also is revealing. Practically all archaeological activity
is that of tomb-robbing. There is no single recorded
instance of the excavation of a pre-Hellenic habitation-
site, none of a habitation-site of the archaic Hellenic
period and only two near cities, at Kouklia in the
Paphos district where research was mainly confined to
the sanctuary and at Salamis. Obviously the Cesnola
tradition still throve and tombs and sanctuaries were
the main objectives. Thus there were many serious
blanks in the archaeological history of Cyprus. There
was no trace of habitation recorded before the Bronze
Age, for none had been found. Of the Bronze Age
nothing was known except from the evidence of tombs.
No stratified site had been properly excavated. Of
the Early Iron Age nothing was known except from
tombs, while for the Orientalizing and early Archaic
periods scholars had to depend on tomb finds and
sanctuary finds, and nothing at all was known of the
manner in which the Kings of Cyprus lived in their
kingdoms, this last perhaps the most serious gap of all.

How it comes about that until the last five years
our knowledge of the archaeology of the Cypriot
kingdoms has remained a complete blank is hard to
explain. The preoccupation with tombs and sanctuaries seems largely to have diverted interest from

other periods and sites. And yet it was known from the evidence of Cypriot coins as well as from other sources that there were at least ten kingdoms in the seventh century, while as late as the fourth century B.C. eight of these had survived, and one new one had been formed.[1] And yet, oddly enough, no archaeologist or antiquarian had made any serious attempt to find out in what respect, archaeologically, these kingdoms differed from the ordinary Greek city-state of the mainland. In view of the extraordinary capacity for survival of these kingdoms, it is the more regrettable that some such investigation was not undertaken ; a fuller knowledge of their organization and adornment might well have thrown more light on their origins. Who were these kings ? The names of so many of them survive and their activities are so evident at all periods of the kingdoms, that we are tempted to ask how they came to last right through a period when Greek political thought had firmly banished all forms of monarchy in other parts of the Greek world. Were these kings politically the descendants of the kings of the Homeric kingship, and so derived from as remote a period as the Homeric Age of Cyprus ? if they were of later origin, how did their monarchies come about ? did they live in palaces or were they little more than ' leaders of the people ' ? were they all priest-kings like the Cinyrads of Paphos [2] and, if so, were they in any way connected in type with the priest-kings of the Minoan world ?

To some of these questions archaeology could have

[1] Hill, *B.M. Cat. of Coins*, *Cyprus*, p. xix, and Diodorus, xvi, 42.
[2] Hill, op. cit., p. lxii.

given direct answers and to others indirect answers. But nothing was either sought for or found which could have illuminated problems so numerous and so important.

But more serious depredations occurred than those which neglect and lack of surveillance were able unaided to produce. In 1879 the Government filled up the marsh which had formed on the site of the ancient harbour of Kition, with ballast taken from what was then thought to be the acropolis of that city ! excavations at the supposed site of Marion carried out in 1885 led to the opening of 441 tombs, the sale of the collection of antiquities so formed by auction in Paris in 1886 (less the third part assigned to the Government), and so to the dispersal of a highly important group of finds. No official report of these excavations was published by the excavators.[1]

The long and dismal story can be continued almost indefinitely, and it were better not to dwell on it. Cesnola at least worked under a Turkish domination. Subsequent vandals had no such excuse ; indeed the Government itself, as in the instance at Larnaka (Kition) just referred to, was the ringleader in many cases. But it was under Turkish rule that medieval churches of Famagusta were torn down and sold as building material to the architects of the hotels and quays of Port Said,[2] while the refectory, intact and in perfect condition, at Bellapais, was used as a miniature rifle-range for the instruction of British troops, the

[1] Myres, *Catalogue*, p. 9.
[2] Gunnis, *Historic Cyprus*, p. 89. Similar depredation occurred at Soloi (idem, p. 257) where the Greco-Roman city was then looted.

memory of this barbaric usage surviving to this day in the pitted walls of its eastern end, pock-marked with bullet-holes.[1]   In the last ten years also the fortifications of Nicosia have steadily been destroyed, both by the driving of roads through them and that the valuable blocks of ashlar might be put by government authorities to some more practical purpose.

In 1933, however, various searchlights of inquiry were focused on the archaeological situation of the island and a first attempt was made to instil both into the British Government and into English people in general the fact that in the Crown Colony of Cyprus Great Britain possessed a property in whose narrow limits were to be found remains of the highest importance and value ;   that the archaeology of Cyprus had been badly mismanaged for half a century of British ownership, and that, even so, what archaeological organization there was had ignored most of the medieval remains and failed to find out much of the classical and prehistoric periods, in which most of the researchers were expert.   The Cyprus Exploration Fund had made a valiant attempt to excavate on sound historical and scientific lines, but for the most part had failed to escape from the lure of tomb-robbing and sanctuary-gutting that had obsessed Cesnola and his followers.   Hogarth, in his *Devia Cypria*, the result of a tourist-travel in 1888, had collected a heterogeneous mass of information rather in the manner of an eighteenth-century traveller. What he discovered was of no great importance and his absence of interest in many periods of history is

[1] Gunnis, *Historic Cyprus*, p. 214.

striking. The time he spent refuting Cesnola's in-
accuracies might have been better spent discovering
sites of the regal palaces. It was left to Professor
J. L. Myres to bring order out of chaos by his re-
organization of the Museum and publication of the
Catalogue, the first real and valuable contribution to
Cypriot archaeology, cautious and reliable, and of
great service to archaeologists to-day ; the work of
Max Ohnefalsch-Richter was also of high value and
his excavations were well-conducted by the standards
of his times. The British Museum carried out many
excavations [1] in every case rather to enrich the collections of the Museum than to add to knowledge by
scientific excavation. The richest finds thus made for
the Museum were those from the cemetery of Enkomi,
near Salamis. But the excavations were such that
much evidence was lost and much damage done.[2]
Other museums also hastened to enrich their collections
and the Berlin Museum, the Louvre and even the
South Kensington Museum, which is not a museum
of archaeology, were each authorized to excavate and
depart with the products, or at least with two-thirds
of them.

[1] By Sir Charles Newton at Akhna in 1882, a sanctuary ; over
a thousand votive figures found. At Alambra in 1883 (two
necropoleis) ; at Dali in 1883 (a necropolis) ; various excavations
at Kition 1879–82 (necropoleis) ; at Kurion in 1895 (Mycenaean
necropolis) ; at Mari in 1881 (necropolis) ; at Ormidhia near
Larnaka in 1882 (sanctuary) ; at Salamis and Enkomi in 1880
and 1882 and again in 1896 when the rich Mycenaean necropolis
was found.

[2] See *Swedish Cyprus Expedition*, I, p. 466, and Evans in *J.A.I.*,
1900, p. 201, n.2., for comments on the methods of the excavators of Enkomi.

The pace of excavation and looting slowed down
after 1896 and Cyprus was for a time forgotten as
new regions were opened up. This date happens to
coincide with that in which Crete made its début as
a new centre of research, and in consequence Cyprus
fades out of the picture. The gold rush had gone
elsewhere. From 1896 to 1913 little more of importance was done and on the basis of previous work
archaeologists had come to certain general conclusions. The course of its prehistory seemed fairly
clear. So vast an accumulation of objects had been
found in the innumerable cemeteries and sanctuaries
that it was possible at least to generalize as to the
course of development of art in the island. The
nature of the antiquities and the artistic conservatism
of Cypriots in the past made this an easy task. The
Mycenaean Age was seen to have qualities which,
archaeologically, made Cyprus exceedingly interesting, but still, a backwater, to which, as the Mycenaean
world crashed, fled whatever was left. It was believed
that Cyprus had an importance in this period solely
as a refuge. For the classical age there was little to
say. An analysis of its art, judging from the specimens found, showed an attractive Archaic period
which rapidly became stereotyped until it faded away
in the fifth century and finally touched depths of
banality and boredom not seen in Greek art elsewhere.
No wonder that archaeologists now began to look
elsewhere. Crete and a reviving interest in Greek
art of the Orientalizing period led researchers off into
new pastures.

A fresh start was begun in 1913, with the help of

M. Markides, the Director of the Museum. But his illness and the outbreak of the War finally put a stop to Cypriot research and it was not until 1927 that a new interest revived. And it is to foreigners excavating in our Crown colony that the main credit must be due for the revival of interest that has again revivified research in the island. A Swedish expedition, armed with the fullest terms of reference and prepared for a long campaign of years, set to work in 1927. The main results of this extensive campaign are now being published.[1] But it was not merely that a revived interest in Cyprus had grown up. What has really happened is that at last it is possible to see Cyprus in its true perspective. The immense stimulus that resulted from the discoveries in Crete led to a general increase of research into Mycenaean origins. This in turn led to the renewed excavation of Mycenae itself in 1920-3, to wide mainland explorations and finally the whole course of Mycenaean research found itself insensibly turning eastwards. This has recently led to the renewed excavations of Troy, abandoned after the final excavations of Doerpfeld in 1893-4. Then in 1931 came the astonishing discoveries at Ras-el-Shamra where it was found that Mycenaean intrusion had reached even here as far east as Syria. Cyprus thus came to take on a new interest. A re-reading of Homeric history, and the revelations of the Hittite texts from Boghaz Keui published in 1924 suggested that Cyprus was in fact a secondary centre of Mycenaean development and a place of concentration for

---

[1] *The Swedish Cyprus Expedition : 1927-1931.* Two volumes of text and plates, and two more to come.

enterprises in Anatolia and Syria. The whole My-
cenaean-Minoan question was assuming a new aspect.
Consequently it was not surprising to find M. Schaeffer,
the excavator of Ras-el-Shamra, coming to Cyprus in
1933 to find out if there was any connexion between
his site and the Mycenaean sites of the island. Renewed excavations at damaged Enkomi were the
sequel. American enterprise has followed and the
classical site of Curium is now under excavation again.
Cyprus is having a revival of popularity mainly because forty years of general research have shown that
there are more problems to solve than the first
excavators dreamed of and that Cyprus holds the clue
to many which concern areas larger than the 3584
square miles of the island. That the first excavators
of tombs and sanctuaries did not realize this is not their
fault. It is merely one of the consequences of the
progress of knowledge.

What these new problems are and whether they
can all be solved in Cyprus will be discussed in the
following chapters.

In the matter of formal archaeology and archaeological classification Cyprus has been well served.
Its coins have been admirably investigated and classified by Six, Babelon and Hill ; [1] its pottery arranged
and brought into order by Myres ; its sculpture faithfully, but not fully, dealt with by various authorities.[2]

[1] See G. F. Hill, *B.M. Cat. of Coins, Cyprus*, p. xviii, n. 2, for a
numismatic bibliography.
[2] Myres, *Cesnola Cat.* : F. N. Pryce, *B.M. Cat. of Sculpture*,
I, ii, 1931 : A. W. Lawrence, *J.H.S.*, 1926, p. 163 ; also a valuable account of its pottery by Gjerstad in *C.V.A.*, 16.

CHAPTER II

PREHISTORIC CYPRUS

THE study of the prehistory of Cyprus has suffered from the uneven accumulation of evidence. It has also until recently lacked the evidence provided by a systematic stratigraphical study of habitation-sites. For the Early and Middle Bronze Age there was available the enormous mass of evidence from thousands of tombs, almost none at all from village sites or fortress-settlements, and little has been done to trace the gradual development of artefacts. For the Late Bronze Age, which can be equated with a Mycenaean Age, the material of superlative quality accessible to all students has been the subject of considerable controversy : the evidence available has been treated too often rather as evidence in support of a thesis instead of being considered from a strictly Cypriot point of view. Too often archaeologists have tried to fit the Cypriot Mycenaean evidence into a preconceived theory of Mycenaean activity in the Levant instead of drawing from the evidence the conclusions which might go to make a theory. This is the defect of much of the recent Swedish work in the island.

One of the strangest features of the study of Cypriot prehistory has been the early lack of success in the

identification of a Neolithic period.   Professor Myres
in 1899 [1] states

the Stone Age has left, so far as is known, but very slight traces
in Cyprus.   Palaeolithic implements have not been recorded at
all. . . .   Neolithic implements are also very rare.   No tombs
or other deposits of the Stone Age have been discovered at all
hitherto.   In particular, there is no distinct Stone Age pottery.

By 1914 no further information was to hand and
the same archaeologist writes,[2] ' of the Neolithic Age
no sites have been found '.   No mention of pre-
Bronze Age culture is made in Gjerstad's *Studies
on Prehistoric Cyprus*, published as recently as 1926.
Alleged megalithic monuments have for the most part
been satisfactorily identified as historical or even
modern [3] and the sole instance where a case might
conceivably be made out for the existence of a trilithon
of the Stonehenge type must remain hypothetical :
I refer to the interior sacred stones of the Tekke of
Umm Haram near the Salt Lake at Larnaka.[4]   The
extreme consideration paid by government authorities
to Turkish religious susceptibilities makes it impossible
to examine these stones, which are enclosed in a metal
grille and covered with green silk.   I have myself
made as close an examination of this strange relic as
is possible, but what is at present allowed is totally
insufficient to make it possible even to guess at the
nature of the stones.   Nor do Turkish records or

---

[1] *Catalogue of the Cyprus Museum*, p. 13.   In P.W. it is noted
that ' Neolithische Keramik und Gräber fehlen '.

[2] *Cesnola Catalogue*, p. xxviii.

[3] In P.W., *s.v.* Kypros, p. 83, Cobham in *J.R. Asiatic Soc*, 1897.

[4] Storrs, *Handbook*, p. 88, Oberhummer, p. 436.

legends give the smallest assistance. With such difficulties scientific archaeology cannot hope to compete.

In the whole of the Cesnola Collection there is no
single fragment of a pottery which could be identified
as pre-Bronze Age, and no Neolithic article has been
included.

That earlier workers should have failed to detect
Neolithic sites and artefacts is odd enough, but that
the elaborate Swedish expedition which set forth to
identify all possible sites and periods should virtually
have failed is still stranger. But such are the fortunes
of war in archaeological research. That the Swedish
archaeologists strongly suspected an early Neolithic
period in Cyprus is indicated by their tabulation of the
settlement-site on the rock in the sea known as Petra
tou Limniti [1] as what they call ' Pre-Neolithic '. But
archaeologically this term means nothing at all and
is mere definition by negation. The classification is
explained as being due to the fact that no trace of
pottery was found, and the excavators assume an age
which they cannot call Palaeolithic because the artefacts are clearly not of that age, but which they believe
to be characterized by a mode of life in which stone
alone was employed as a medium of manufacture.
Such a period, which is neither Palaeolithic nor Neolithic and certainly not Bronze Age, belongs to a
Wonderland of archaeology. It would have been
better if the excavators had noted the site and its finds
and then filed it for future use as knowledge accumulated. In fact, as will be seen, the discovery of circular
hut-foundations suggests that Petra tou Limniti can

[1] Gjerstad, *Swedish Cyprus Expedition*, I, p. 1, and Pl. VII.

3

now be certainly classified as a site of the early Neolithic Age, while the subsequent discoveries at Khirokhitia identify it with the culture of that site. The
same expedition also made the tentative identification
of a full Neolithic period by the discovery at Lapethos
and at Kythraea of settlements containing meagre
elements of a supposed Neolithic Age, consisting of
painted pottery of a type not hitherto recorded, and
stone axes. As early as 1898 some stray fragments
from Kalavasos had reached the British Museum.
But they were not then certainly identifiable as
Neolithic.[1]

Cyprus never fails in surprises, and in 1933 M.
Dikaios, the Curator of the Cyprus Museum, identified and excavated the first large Neolithic site in the
island at Erimi, not far from Limassol on the southern
coast.[2]

The actual site is on low ground some three miles
from the shore on the banks of a small but never-
failing river. The area covered by the settlement
comprises several acres and the population must have
been great. The duration of the site also must have
been considerable, for the depth of the deposit is
several metres. The principal characteristics of this
wholly new culture revealed by these excavations are
as follows.

---

[1] *S.C.E.*, I, 13 ff. and 277 ff. Plates, IX, X, XII, XIII, and
B.M. Cat. of Vases, I, i, p. 14, fig. 23, and Dikaios *Annual
Report*, 1934, p. 6.
[2] *J.H.S.*, 1933, part ii, p. 294 ; *Antiquity*, 1934, p. 86 ; *Illus-
trated London News*, 19 Jan., 1935. *Cyprus* : Department of
Antiquities, Report No. 2, 1934, p. 5.

The houses were placed closely together and were always (as far as present evidence goes) circular in shape and built of large unworked stones. The roof was supported by a pole from the centre. The inhabitants of this large village made implements of chipped and polished flint and stone instruments of bone and ornaments of steatite and clay. They buried their dead in a crouching position outside the houses. And they made a magnificent pottery. The vessels are often of great size and are of two main fabrics—white-painted and red-slip wares. The white-painted ware is 'made of a hard, gritty, brownish clay, which is covered with a fine white or buff slip on which painted patterns of a geometrical and sometimes very elaborate style are applied'. 'The red-slip ware is similar in make to the white-painted ware, with the difference that the surface is covered with a thin red or brown wash'. The red-slip ware seems to precede in time the other, though both exist contemporaneously in the later stages of the settlement. The shapes are simple and the vessels all hand-made. Large beakers and ovoid jars seem to predominate.

Since this site was opened other Neolithic sites have been identified. The most important is the site of Khirokhitia on the south coast midway between Larnaka and Limassol. Here Mr. Dikaios has found an extensive settlement of an earlier phase of the Neolithic period than at Erimi. The inhabitants made their vessels of stone, of the type found previously by the Swedes at Petra tou Limniti. Their culture seems to have been ignorant of ceramic or to have employed perishable material for their vessels, except in the case of those made of stone. But the upper levels of Khirokhitia produced red incised pottery of the type found at the bottom levels of Erimi. It is thus now possible to establish the broad outlines of the Neolithic period. The whole period, on the assumption that the Bronze Age began about 3000 B.C., would be roughly divided as follows :

4000–3500 : The phase represented by Khirokhitia, except in its upper levels.

3500 : The phase represented by the red incised pottery from upper Khirokhitia and the lowest levels of Erimi. Such pottery has also been found at a site Sotira, near Limassol.

3500–3000 : The Erimi-culture as a whole.

3000 : Traces of a contact with the Bronze Age perhaps to be seen in the Swedish finds at Lapethos and Kythraea. But this is uncertain.

Other sites where Neolithic elements have been identified are Aghios Epiktetos, and Karavas in the Kyrenia district, Meladhia and Tremithousa in the Paphos district, Dhikomo near Kythraea and Phrenaros, Pyla, Alaminos, Kalavasos and Sotira in the south.[1]

It would be rash to generalize on the present state of our knowledge for this period, but it is clear that the island was populated by a thriving Neolithic popula-

[1] Two steatite idols of very fine and skilful workmanship are in the Nicosia Museum. They are said to come from Pomos in the Paphos district. They are apparently Neolithic. See *Dept. of Antiq.*, Report No. 2, 1934, p. 16.

tion for a very long time and it is also clear that this
culture had little connexion with the earliest Bronze
Age of the island. Indeed the most remarkable fact
of all is the almost complete difference between the
Neolithic fabrics and those of the first Bronze Age.
Here is a prehistoric settlement of the island that trans-
mitted nothing to the next age. It was either exterminated or else had died a natural death before the
age of metals began. Neither the circular houses
nor the shapes, patterns and fabrics of the pottery
find an echo in any subsequent period. This is the
more remarkable in view of the enormous power
of transmission perceptible in subsequent Cypriot
history.

As far as present knowledge goes, it is impossible
to make any suggestions as to the origin of this fine
and not unlovely Cypriot Neolithic pottery. In so
far as any comparisons can be made I should be
inclined to say that it resembles the fine white-slip
wares of the western Mediterranean. The pottery of
Molfetta and other sites in Southern Italy [1] is similar
in fabric. In any case the Cypriot Neolithic wares
bear no resemblance at all to anything known in
Syria or Egypt. Still less do they resemble the wares
of the Middle East. Both the thickness of the wares
and the thickness and polish of the white slip suggest
comparisons only with North Anatolian wares, and
the red-slip wares resemble similar wares from Central

---

[1] A comparison with Thessalian wares naturally follows. It
had in fact been previously suggested in *B.M. Cat.*, p. 15. See
Dikaios in *Ill. Lon. News*, 26.12.36. For the finds at Khirokhitia
see this same publication.

and South Anatolia.   The problem remains and only
further research will throw light on the origin of the
makers of this first Cypriot ceramic, which, artistic-
ally, is superior in quality to any fabric before the
white wares of the Late Bronze Age.   It is also notable
that the essentially Cypriot-Anatolian gourd-forms
are largely absent from the repertoire of these Neolithic potters.   All we can say at the moment is that
the Neolithic Cypriots seem to have handed down
almost nothing to posterity from their culture.

The change to a Bronze Age was thus abrupt.
Whether there was an interval during which Cyprus
remained uninhabited, or whether there was a super-
imposition of Bronze Age peoples, endowed with a
knowledge of metals upon the indigenous Neolithic
folk, can only be solved by a close analysis of stratigraphical evidence on habitation-sites.   At Erimi no
trace of Bronze Age levels has so far been found super-
imposed on the earlier site.   The first remains found
below the modern soil are all Neolithic.   Some testimony to the longevity of Cypriot memory may be
gathered from the fact that the very name of the
village which stands on this ancient site, suggests that
for countless generations the abandoned settlement of
the earliest known Cypriot site preserved the name
which it may have borne after its first abandonment
—Erimi means ' the deserted place ' [1] given to it when
Greek was first spoken.

With the dawn of a Bronze Age in the island we

[1] A particularly inappropriate title for the rich fields and vine-
yards, watered by a good rivulet, situated in one of the most
fertile parts of the island.

are at once plunged into archaeological controversy.
The earliest Cypriot Bronze Age wares have marked
and distinct characteristics. But Professor Myres
wisely hints at the possibility of a pre-Bronze Age
settlement of the island, and points out that in the
earliest Bronze Age tombs at Lapethos ' there are
already two distinct racial types '.[1]

But the evidence provided by the tombs of the
Early Bronze Age—and tombs must suffice, for no
habitation-site has yet been excavated [2]—shows that
the Cypriots of this time were living a life which had
much in common with that of Anatolia, Egypt and
Syria. Myres remarks that the characteristic Cypriot
red-polished pottery appears in the island, in its characteristic gourd and skin forms, fully developed and
completely competent. There are no stages of steady
development. He explains this by the supposition—
and it is difficult to devise any other—that ' the art
of pot-making was introduced in an advanced phase
from the mainland into an island culture which had
used only perishable vessels before : the sudden
appearance of a fine fabric of pottery would thus be
fully explained '.[3] The new fact that Neolithic
pottery of great ceramic skill and no affinities with
gourd and skin shapes had been previously manufac-
tured makes the hypothesis previously suggested here
more probable—that there was a gap of non-occupa-

[1] *Cesnola Catalogue*, p. xxviii, and L. H. D. Buxton in
J.R.A.I., 1920, p. 184.
[2] Myres had examined a Bronze Age settlement at Kalopsida.
J.H.S., xvii, p. 138.
[3] *Cesnola Catalogue*, ibid.

tion between the ancient Neolithic and the preliminary
Bronze Age. The aboriginals whom the first Bronze
Age people found in residence may well have lost
their ceramic skill by degeneration, and reverted to
gourds and skins. For that some aboriginals were
there seems indicated by the anthropological evidence
of the earliest Bronze Age graves. Myres's theory of
the introduction of a new fabric ready-made and fully
equipped presumes the arrival into the island of new
people. The Bronze Age thus at once heralds the
first certain intrusion into Cyprus of external peoples.
This does not, however, imply any necessary racial
change. The Bronze Age people of Cyprus, as far
as we can reconstruct their character, were pastoral
and agricultural people who inhabited the lowlands
and plains, and their pastoral character is indicated by
the prevalence of ladles and open bowls with spouts,
which are the typical furniture of dairymen.[1] Corn-
grinders and querns are also common. Axe-heads,
dagger-blades and scrapers are the commonest objects
in metal. They bury their dead and never cremate,
and the richness of their burial furnishings presupposes
a view of the after-life which considered it as in some
sort a replica of this.

The problem remains of the place of origin of the
new ideas, and of whether these new ideas certainly
imply a new people who brought them.

One plain fact is useful at the outset. The forms
of this new pottery of the Early Bronze Age are
nowhere found so abundantly or in so much variety
as in Cyprus. A second fact is equally important—

[1] Myres, *Cyprus Catalogue*, p. 15.

all this pottery is hand-made and the potter's wheel is unknown. We can therefore say with tolerable safety that the new pottery was not invented first in Egypt, for there wheel-made pottery was made at this time. Nor can we say that this Cypriot pottery originated in Syria or Anatolia, although the typical Cypriot forms were recognized by Cesnola and Schliemann to be related to the Troadic shapes. Comparisons have been made between the Cypriot pottery and that of Libyan sites, as at Ballas and Naqada in Egypt. But here, while the technique and colour is much the same, the shapes are totally different, those of the Libyan potters depending on types of stone vessels and only rarely on gourd or skin shapes.

On the other hand, there remains from these com-parisons—and they are the only possible comparisons with Cypriot pottery of the Bronze Age—the definite conclusions that Egyptian, Anatolian and Cypriot pottery had in common the technique of texture, colour and surface. In shape the comparison is not so close. Syria to some extent links up between Egypt and Anatolia, and so gives us a compact Levantine area in which a red-polished ware developed. The northern limits seem to be the shores of the Black Sea.

How then are we to find out where Cyprus stands in this area ? whether the island was the originator of the whole pottery technique, or whether the tech-nique started outside the island and reached the island, which then took on a technique only, without in-heriting a repertoire of shapes ?

Gjerstad's [1] view, based on that of Ohnefalsch-Richter, seems moderate and sensible. He assumes that the closest connexion is between Cyprus and South Anatolia [2] where both shapes and clay and colour show affinity in the pottery. There were, he thinks, two Bronze Age areas of culture, Anatolia and Cyprus, of which one separated off from the other. [3] The sudden appearance of the Bronze Age wares in Cyprus and our certain knowledge now that it had not developed from a Neolithic origin, makes it almost certain that it was the Cypriot branch which broke off from Anatolia ; in other words, the Cypriot Bronze Age was derivative from a Bronze Age which had pre-existed in Anatolia and had had a general spread all over the Levant from Libya to Phrygia.

What made Cyprus the goal of a new development of the Levantine Bronze Age has yet to be explained, but the usual suggestion is that, with the dawn of metallurgy, came the demand for new producing areas. As such Cyprus was the richest copper region of the Levant, the nearest alternative source being Sinai, which had supplied Egypt from the First Dynasty. [4] Once this intensive development of a new area occurred, the increase of Cypriot activity, which

[1] *Studies on Prehistoric Cyprus*, p. 297 ff.

[2] Although no certain importations of the Cypriot red ware to Anatolia or of Anatolian wares to Cyprus are recorded. Gjerstad, op. cit., p. 296.

[3] Op. cit., p. 300. ' South-western Anatolia is thus not " pure Cypriot " but it represents a culture which, so far as hitherto known, shows the closest connexion with the earliest Bronze Age culture on Cyprus.'

[4] Lucas, *Ancient Egyptian Materials and Industries* (1934), p. 156 ff.

HILARION CASTLE ROCK, FROM THE NORTH NEAR KYRENIA
THE FERTILE NORTHERN PLAIN IN THE FOREGROUND

is marked from the very beginning of the Bronze Age, was bound to follow. But against this theory, that the Bronze Age of Cyprus was due in the first instance to the development of its copper mines, is the more solid evidence that the people of the Cypriot Bronze Age were mostly pastoral (see above, p. 28) this at any rate must be taken into account. As the Bronze Age developed the copper mines were certainly worked (see below, p. 122 ff.), but it is improbable that their working coincided with the early stages of the Bronze Age.

The plain fact remains that the first period of intensive Cypriot life begins with the Bronze Age, so intensive that some fragments of its inheritance survive to-day (see p. 4 ff.). The populated area of the island in the Neolithic Age is not yet known, probably the inhabitants were concentrated in a few areas in large and heavily occupied villages. Such at least is the inference from the fact that Neolithic sites are rare enough to have escaped notice for two generations, but when found seen to be large enough to cover an area as large as, say, a small modern Cypriot town such as Athienou. In contrast the Bronze Age settlers were scattered all over the island and lived both in small settlements and in large towns and forts. Cyprus took on a status with the development of the Bronze Age and the whole island, apart from the uplands of volcanic formation in the south-west, was under a fairly intensive cultivation. As was to be expected, the Early Bronze Age is an age of internal development without external contacts. Cyprus is insular and pastoral and not as yet seeking markets outside or welcoming strangers.[1] The Bronze Age settlement perhaps grew up as a mere extension across the Caramanian Straits from southern Asia Minor of an already well-established population of farmers and agriculturists. They just crossed over from the mainland into new pastures.

The main characteristics of the Early Bronze Age are (a) that copper is more prevalent for implements than bronze,[2] (b) painted patterns are unknown on the only pottery fabrics used—a further point which shows the almost complete breach of continuity between the Neolithic and Bronze Age; (c) such patterns as are employed on the pottery are purely geometric and are incised : frequently these patterns are arranged in a disjunctive way[3] over a given surface in a manner which suggests the disjunctive decoration of early Egyptian wares. But for the most part this Early Bronze Age pottery has its patterns arranged in some co-ordinated plan.

(d) There are only two main fabrics of this period, the ubiquitous red-polished ware and a black-polished ware. Substantially both are the same fabric[4] and both have the same coarse gritty clay, but in the one

---

[1] The earliest contacts with foreign lands in the Early Bronze Age are with Syria and Egypt (via Syria) ; see Gjerstad, op. cit., p. 302.

[2] Myres, *Cesnola Catalogue*, p. xxix.

[3] E.g. *Cesnola Catalogue*, Nos. 89–98—a very common class.

[4] See Lucas, *Ancient Egyptian Materials*, p. 321. Some authorities consider the black ware to be of Balkan origin. Gjerstad (op. cit., p. 296) believes it to be a wholly Cypriot ware, only a special technical variety of the Cypriot red ware. That view has long been generally accepted.

case the fine deep crimson-red colour has been achieved by true firing while in the other, by deliberate damping down of the furnace or by the deliberate intrusion of combustible material, the clay has absorbed smoke particles into its structure while red hot.

(e) The shapes are all reminiscent of shapes made in other fabrics than pottery. Gourds, complete with their long necks, or halved, skin shapes and baskets all seem to have suggested both shape and pattern.

(f) All vessels have a convex basal side and so cannot stand motionless on a plane surface. The larger vessels were made to lean against a wall or in a corner, or else in a rough stand ; the smaller had the qualities of tumbler-cups. This more than anything indicates the gourd-origin of the majority of shapes and the curious fact that pottery never had an independent start as pottery in Cyprus, but was always derivative from something else. This is in striking contrast with the Neolithic shapes which are those of pottery uninfluenced to any large extent by the gourd. Neolithic vessels have bases. This point also further emphasizes the breach of continuity between the two ages.

The Middle Bronze Age is distinguished by new experiments in ceramic. Skin-shapes are more influential than gourds and a new white ware, with a matt surface, decorated in a dull red or rich black paint, emerges from these experiments side by side with the usual red-polished wares. Vessels are adapted into quaint animal shapes—a type of vessel probably for ornamental table use—and small and elaborate vessels are now made which are largely to be used by suspension from handles or side-lugs. Slowly the Cypriot potter is trying to experiment and feeling his way, but it is noteworthy that as yet there is no trace of aesthetic appreciation. His wares amuse and interest, but no more. The severe simplicity of Cypriot Neolithic is absent and never does the potter achieve shapes aesthetically admirable like those of Neolithic China or the wares of Cucuteni and Dimini in Europe. The Cypriot potter was small-minded at the start; he preferred fiddling for entertaining shapes and fussing over dull repetitive patterns rather than thinking out bolder ideas or really building up his shapes in true ceramic tradition. No doubt his style had from the first (in the Bronze Age) been severely cramped by the insistence of his customers for pottery imitations of the gourds to which they had been accustomed; but the fact that he only rarely emerged from this dull world and never experienced much ' customer-resistance' shows that he had not in him the stuff of the real ceramist. The whole of the subsequent history of Cypriot ceramic is largely determined by these initial weaknesses.

Implements of true bronze are common in the Middle Bronze Age. Connexions with Egypt are apparent and the stone mace-heads now used in Cyprus may be derived from Egypt or the Middle East, while direct evidence is shown in the import of Egyptian blue beads of the XIIth Dynasty and of Babylonian cylinders of the second half of the third millennium B.C.[1]

Cyprus in the Middle Bronze Age was reaching

[1] Myres, *Cesnola Catalogue*, p. xxix ; Gjerstad, op. cit., p. 303.

out to other lands, but her direction of aim is eastwards and not to the west.[1]   Corresponding imports
of pottery from Syria and Palestine and of ornaments
from Egypt, occur.   She had started her prosperity
with unexpected suddenness.

The foundations of prosperity laid by the Early
Bronze Age Cypriots were built upon so solidly by
their successors of the Middle Bronze Age that soon
Cyprus begins to take a place of importance in the
Levant.   In all probability trade with Egypt was
merely a continuation of the coastal trade with Syria
and Palestine.[2]   A flood of Cypriot exports of pottery
reaches the Syrian shore and Middle Cypriot pottery
reaches even as far south as Nubia, 1,300 kilometres
from the Nile delta.   Cypriot pottery shapes are
actually imitated by Egyptian potters.[3]

It would be wise to preserve the greatest caution
at this point in considering the archaeological evidence.
Archaeologists are too prone to think that if one land
imports the pots of another that there must be some
kind of reciprocal ceramic intercourse.   They all too
often fail to ask why it was that the pots were imported in the first instance.   Pottery in antiquity was
not exported and imported merely to blaze a trail for
subsequent archaeological inquiry.   Pots were seldom
articles of trade in themselves unless they had artistic

[1] Gjerstad, *Studies on Prehistoric Cyprus*, pp. 304–8.   Examples
of Cypriot imports in this period to Palestine, Syria and Egypt.

[2] Ibid., p. 302 and 305.

[3] Gjerstad, op. cit., pp. 322–3.   The further assumption made
here that there were Cypriot factories in Egypt is hazardous in
the extreme.   One is tempted to ask factories of what, for
Cypriot pottery had no intrinsic artistic or other merits.

merits or technical virtues which made them in themselves desirable. Corinthian pottery of the sixth century reached its various and remote destinations mainly because it consisted of small receptacles for precious scents and unguents. But Attic vases for the most part were *objets d'art et de vertu.*

Cypriot pottery, in the Middle Bronze Age, is never of the smallest artistic merit, even by Egyptian ceramic standards; it reached Egypt for some practical reason. Cypriot pots contained something that was wanted in Syria, Palestine and Egypt. Perhaps it was wine, possibly it was scents and unguents. We have no certain knowledge. In any case Cyprus had at last made itself known to the outside world, from which in return came various imports—pottery from Syria and Anatolia, ornaments from Egypt and Babylonia.

The date 1500 is taken for convenience as heralding the beginning of the Late Bronze Age of Cyprus, one of the most deeply interesting periods in the whole history of the island. I propose first to consider the development of this period from a purely ceramic point of view, for it is in the study of its always individual pottery that the island can best exhibit the changes that were now coming over it. Cyprus as seen *from outside* in the Late Bronze Age will be dealt with in a later chapter, for the sources available are numerous and important.

The first outstanding feature of this great period in Cypriot ceramic is the appearance of a wholly new and very striking type of pottery. It is a white ware entirely unlike any previous Cypriot ware in fabric.

The white-painted wares of the Early Bronze Age may perhaps have suggested it, but the actual clay is different from that of any other Cypriot fabric except the Base Ring ware,[1] so much so that we must be quite certain that it is Cypriot in origin and not imported from elsewhere. To this suspicion it can be replied at once that, although this white-slip ware is in fact found widespread over the Levant and the Aegean, the enormous preponderance of examples comes from Cyprus itself. This argument, usually unsafe, can be accepted here, for the extent of excavation in recent years has been so considerable that the home of this ware would almost certainly have been found by now, had it been made outside Cyprus.

In itself this ware, one of the few attractive prehistoric wares ever made in the island, exhibits its essentially Cypriot nature in its close adherence to non-ceramic origins. As in many previous and subsequent Cypriot wares also the paint, usually sepia, is matt and not lustrous. In the opinion of Professor Myres[2] the shapes and patterns alike are almost exclusively derived from leather work. Even the handles imitate the kind of handles, with a wooden core, which would be necessary to attach to leather bottles and jugs and bowls. The painted lines and geometric strips which adorn the sides of the vessels of this fabric also follow closely the seams which would hold together the several parts of leathern vessels. Every element of these vases is, in fact, derivative. Again the Cypriot potter shows his dislike of pottery for its own sake, a deeply-seated prejudice.

[1] *Cesnola Catalogue*, p. 32. [2] Idem, loc. cit.

4

The shapes of these vessels follow no rigid classification. As in the previous age the potter was incessantly experimenting and fussing with elaborations of his main repertoire. The long-necked jug and the open bowl with one or two handles alone remain more or less orthodox, especially the bowl, which often unconsciously attains great beauty of form, and is at the same time a practical bowl to use for eating or drinking. The large crater or open-beaker bowl, which is merely the ordinary bowl with a top storey built on it, is another common shape.

With shapes such as these it is obviously impossible to think of their export as receptacles for wine or scents. The fact that this ware does attain to some considerable commercial popularity is almost certainly due to its interesting and attractive appearance. For once Cypriot wares had an intrinsic interest of their own, sufficient to attract buyers. At any rate the spread of these wares is considerable and we meet for the first time now the Cypriot tendency to turn its face westwards as well as east and south. This white-slip ware has been found in Egypt at Tell-el-Amarna, and at Saqqara, in Palestine at Lachish, at Tell Abu Hawam, in Syria at Ras Shamra and at Atchana (in the Orontes valley), westwards at Troy, at Thera in the Cyclades and even on the Acropolis at Athens,[1] and at Tiryns in the Argolid.[2]

The dates of these external finds can be fixed only in

[1] Gjerstad, op. cit., p. 325. Circumstances of its finding are not recorded.

[2] Unpublished: found by Professor Sayce at Tiryns and now in the Ashmolean Museum.

the case of the Tell-el-Amarna and the Theraean finds. The former can be equated with a date of the XVIIIth Dynasty, the latter with a rather less precise Middle Minoan date, for the Theraean fragments were found in a settlement of the Middle Cycladic period in which were strong Minoan elements.

It appears then that Cyprus was in touch with the Aegean before Aegean influences swept over Cyprus, the next phase in its development. There are some slight indications that a trade in the reverse direction existed, the evidence of this being certain rare and perhaps stray finds of Minoan pottery in Cyprus. One fragment of Cretan Kamares ware was found in a grave near Kurion, in uncertain circumstances, as it can hardly belong to the grave, which is of the Late Bronze Age.[1] Two Middle Minoan II fragments are recorded.[2] But no imports are recorded in Crete of Cypriot pottery of the same date.

But the distribution of the white-slip ware is an important landmark in Cypriot history. The people who traded it to the west were the first to give away the secrets of this very self-sufficient island to a world that in the Late Bronze Age was beginning to open out with extraordinary speed. The inhabitants of Greece were now beginning to look for new regions for exploitation, and the information about Cyprus which must have arrived with its pottery was exactly what suited their interests and stirred their curiosity. From now on, Cyprus is not a mere island of the Levant.

At a date at present all too loosely defined, but approximately in the half-century after 1400 B.C.,

[1] Gjerstad, op. cit., p. 308.   [2] Idem, p. 209.

connexions of trade, travel and general intercourse seem to have been established between Cyprus and the widely established Mycenaean world, whose predominance had now replaced that of Crete, after the eclipse of Minoan hegemony. The predisposition for these western contacts had been indicated by the arrival of Cypriot wares in the west, already referred to, and by a just perceptible infiltration eastwards of Minoan fabrics in the third millennium and increasing as the First Late and Second Late Minoan (or Late Helladic) periods emerged.[1] By the time when Mycenaean peoples were fabricating the pottery of the early Third Late Minoan period, of the particular stage of development usually indicated by the term 'Tell-el-Amarna type', Cyprus was at last in touch with the Mycenaean mode of culture. This refers to a type of Mycenaean (or 'Late Minoan III') ceramic which can be given the close date of 1380–65 B.C. imported into Egypt from some Mycenaean producing area not yet certainly identified.[2] The earliest recorded Mycenaean wares of L.M. III found in Cyprus conform to the Amarna types.[3]

From now on Cyprus never loses touch with the

[1] Gjerstad, op. cit., p. 210. Parts of a Late Minoan II jar and bowl.

[2] I prefer caution in this matter because it is as yet quite impossible to say whether the exporting region was the Argolid, Rhodes, Crete, or even Cyprus itself. Archaeologists all too often assume that the Mycenaean imports found in outlying places all derive from the Argolid. There is no proof of any kind that this is so. Until satisfactory kiln-evidence is available judgements in matters of pottery-derivation must be hesitating.

[3] Myres, *Cesnola Catalogue*, p. 46.

western world and culture, and there appears a steady
increase in the island of Mycenaean influences. It
is customary to refer [1] in rather loose terms to the
'Mycenaean colonization of Cyprus', and, as often
as not, to argue back again from this assumption to
show that the Mycenaean wares in Cyprus were imported by the colonists from the mainland of Greece.
But this is a most circular mode of argument and
we must proceed cautiously. The facts are plain.
Amarna types appear in Cyprus almost as soon as the
white-slip ware is first made. Indeed at present there
is no certain evidence that the white-slip ware did in
fact precede the Mycenaean. The arrival of these
Amarna Mycenaean types follows along a line of
importation already suggested to traders by the previous import of M.M. II and L.M. I and II oddments.
But the place of export is uncertain. Crete is suggested for the M.M. II and L.M. I and II wares, but
they are so few that a mere chance contact may
account for them. They may even come from
Egypt, where M.M. II wares were admired and purchased from Crete.[2] The L.M. I. and II wares may
have come either from Greece itself or from Crete
or else have drifted to Cyprus from Rhodes, where
such wares are more numerous.[3] It is wholly unwise

[1] E.g. Evans, *Scripta Minoa*, p. 73 ; Myres, *Cesnola Catalogue*,
p. xxx ; Burn,*Minoans, Philistines and Greeks*, p. 104. I am not
accusing these authors of holding the theory held by Gjerstad.
They use the term 'colonization'; others interpret it to imply
'importation' of pottery.

[2] Evans, *Palace of Minos*, I, p. 248 ff.

[3] Rhodes appears to have acted as a clearing-house for Cretan
wares of the Palace style and for early Mainland wares. Tomb

to predicate a commercial contact between Cyprus and the mainland of Greece on such loose evidence. All we can say is that Cyprus was in touch with peoples who were acquainted with the Mycenaean mode of life. No more specific inference is possible.

The Amarna types of L.M. III wares are numerous enough to assume a real trade connexion, but again, we cannot safely say where the contact was made. Egypt again may have been an intermediary, and the contact may not necessarily be a direct one. We cannot even be certain that both at Amarna and in Cyprus the wares were not made by immigrant potters, though this is an unlikely theory.

What is certain is that, once these early L.M. III wares were known to Cypriots, they created a fashion for Mycenaean pottery which remained one of the most distinctive characteristics of Cypriot taste for several hundred years. From now on to the end of the Bronze Age the sole painted wares in use in Cyprus, besides the white-slip ware and the base-ring ware, were wares either almost indistinguishable from what in mainland Greece and Crete are usually called Mycenaean, or else versions of wares of these types which are clearly related so closely to Mycenaean as to be considered ceramically wholly dependent upon them.

xix at the site Moschu Vounara contained a fine beaker-goblet with one handle decorated with a single design of a ' double axe flower ' and a jug, both of pure L.M. II style. Tomb xviii at the same site contains a large three-handled jar decorated with vine-leaf designs derivative from the Palace style. Tomb xxxi contains a sword pommel, hardly later than L.M. III A made of Laconian green porphyry. This suggests a direct mainland connexion.

PLATE III

CYPRIOT VESSELS OF THE MYCENAEAN PERIOD
(*Nicosia Museum*)

1   2

The appearance of the earliest type of Mycenaean ware may, as has just been suggested, be due to a trade with Egypt. It may equally be due to trade and intercourse direct with Mycenaean centres. It does not necessarily presuppose a colonization of Cyprus from the west. But the enormous quantities of the true Mycenaean wares—what are technically to-day classified as L.M. III A or L.M. III B—force us at once to decide the thorny problem which arises. Here we come up against a flat contradiction, not only of authorities among themselves but even in the various views of one authority.

Hitherto, and before the bulk of the recent Swedish researches in the island were carried out, the term ' Cypro-Minoan ' or ' Cypro-Mycenaean ' has been used to describe those Mycenaean or ' Mycenaeanizing ' wares which did not carry on them the stamp of direct importations or exact local replicas of Mycenaean fabrics. It was thought that there was a school of imitative ceramic in Cyprus which copied, as was done in so many places, the prototypes of the Mycenaean world. Professor Myres classifies as ' Cypro-Mycenaean ' those wares which ' show by the peculiarities of their form and decoration that they represent a local " Cypro-Mycenaean " fabric with a well-marked style of its own '.[1] The same authority also calls attention to a fact previously noted and recognized that paintings depicting chariot-scenes are very popular in Cyprus (see below, p. 44, n. 3) as the decoration of the largest vessels, usually craters or amphorae. He thinks that, in addition to the fact

[1] *Cesnola Catalogue*, p. 47.

that these chariot-scenes do occur with greater frequency in Cyprus than elsewhere on vessels of Mycenaean or 'Mycenaeanizing' type, their style 'has many local peculiarities which mark it as a local Cypriot school, derived from that of Late Minoan Crete and probably to be dated about 1350 B.C.'.[1] Gjerstad, in his first studies on Cyprus,[2] rejects the whole theory without any hesitation. He does not believe that any of these wares, except for certain sub-Mycenaean wares, were made in the island, but that all were imports.[3] Here then is a flat contradiction. Myres,

[1] *Cesnola Catalogue*, p. 48. Cf. Gjerstad, *Studies on Prehistoric Cyprus*, p. 219.

[2] Op. cit., pp. 218-20 and p. 326. ' So far as the present material shows, all the Aegean ware found in Cyprus must be considered as imported.'

[3] He rejects the view that the chariot-scenes are more popular in Cyprus than on the mainland (p. 219) and assumes that such scenes were derived from Minoan and Early Mycenaean palace-frescoes by the vase-painters. Such frescoes were not, he thinks, accessible to Cypriot painters, hence all the chariot-scene vases are imports. E. J. Forsdyke, in *Essays in Aegean Archaeology*, p. 31, accepts Gjerstad's view and publishes a fine Mycenaean vase from Maroni which shows a scene of galloping goats. It is based, he thinks, on a fresco of a period antecedent to Mycenaean intrusion into Cyprus and so could not have been made in the island. In date it is L.M. III A. But this view, as expressed by both authorities, is based on a pure assumption, namely that vase-painters deliberately drew from existing frescoes. For this there is no proof at all. It is much more probable that when fresco-painting began to decay, the artists who would otherwise have been fresco-painters, took to painting pots and carried with them a degenerate style derived from earlier fresco styles. Such artists may well have emigrated to Cyprus and carried on their art there. The facts that count are (1) that a majority of chariot-scene vases,

PLATE IV

PAINTED PANEL FROM A CYPRIOT MYCENAEAN CRATER SHOWING
MINOAN LADIES RENDERED IN THE MANNER OF FRESCO-PAINTING
(*British Museum*)

identifies certain wares as hardly distinguishable from Mycenaean but nevertheless local, as well as a large class of obviously local imitations of true Mycenaean wares. Gjerstad classifies everything that resembles Mycenaean ware as imported except the obviously local copies, usually to be distinguished by their coarse clay and dull paint. Myres's view compels us to presuppose a colonization of the island in the fourteenth century by bodies of ' Mycenaeans ' who brought with them the knowledge of the wheel and the technique of their own special wares. One must also assume that his view presupposes that they also manipulated the clay of Cyprus in such a way as to make it indistinguishable from that used for the mainland wares.

and vases with similar pictorial scenes, are actually found in Cyprus ; (2) that the size of almost all these pictorial vessels is so great that they exceed a size convenient for transport (see below, p. 51), (3) that several vases of this pictorial type show in the scattered and ' uncomposed ' nature of their designs a characteristic which is continuously Cypriot in all periods, prehistoric or historic and very markedly unlike the compact composition of mainland Mycenaean vases. This ' uncomposed ' style has been analysed by Myres in *Essays in Aegean Archaeology*, p. 87, where he says of it that it covers a period from the ' Late Minoan decline in the twelfth century to the sixth century or (including the white-painted and polychrome examples) to the fourth and third '. Many of the chariot-scene vases specifically show these qualities of ' uncomposition ' (as that published by Nilsson, *Homer and Mycenae*, pl. 56, our Pl. V, 1). Cyprus was the home of ' loose ' painting on vases. Vases, like that published by Forsdyke, are not ' uncomposed ' and represent the work of earlier immigrants trained in the fresco-schools. The ' uncomposed ' designs are probably the work of local artists of Cypriot origin and tradition. This is the view of Waçe in *C.A.H.*, vol. I (Plates), p. 178, in his

Gjerstad, on the other hand,[1] impressed by the similarity of clay in the true 'Mycenaean' wares of the island to that of the mainland wares, draws the sweeping conclusion that all such wares were imports from Greece and evades difficulties such as that suggested by Myres, that the chariot-scenes are peculiar to Cyprus, by flat denial. 'As we have seen,' he says, 'the Mycenaean ware was imported and, in spite of the great quantity, it does not give reason to assume a Greek colonization of Cyprus.' Again,[2] 'the Mycenaean ware in Cyprus signifies not a Greek colonization . . . but a definite orientation towards the West'.

In other words, Myres believes that large bodies of colonists came over from mainland Greece in Mycenaean times and settled in Cyprus. Hence most of the Mycenaean pottery of later types found there was made in the island for and by these peoples and not imported. Gjerstad, on the other hand, without committing himself to the general truth or otherwise of a Mycenaean immigration to the island, thinks at

remarks on a typical 'uncomposed' Cypriot vessel where, as he says, the design is 'scattered about in the field in a disconnected manner'.

[1] Op cit, p. 220.

[2] p. 327. He seems to contradict his own theory of imports when he says (ibid.) : 'The Mycenaean importation makes the assumption of Mycenaean factories along the Cyprian coast very plausible.' This would bring him to Myres's view of colonies, but I think that for *factories* we should read *ports* or *emporia* in the true Greek sense, mere places of import. This confusion, like some others in his book, is solely due to ambiguities in the English.

least that the pottery is no evidence for it. Myres's theory is an inference from the nature of the pottery.

It would be easy to take sides in this controversy were it not for the fact that Gjerstad denies his own thesis in his later work. In his two large volumes that contain the results up to date of the campaign, he brings into use an entirely new classification for the bulk of the 'Mycenaean' wares. He classifies them as 'Levanto-Mycenaean'. The very term so used presupposes much of Myres's general view, for it is an attempt to evade a blunt repetition of his original 'import' theory. If these wares, which he had in his previous work classified as Mycenaean, are now to be considered as Mycenaean wares made in the Levant (which seems to be the correct implication of the term), then his original theory is clearly discarded. But this is not a very satisfactory way of informing the archaeological world that he no longer believes his first *credo*.

Taken as a whole the problem admits of solution, if considered with less *a priori* bias. The facts are simple. They are as follows :

(*a*) Small quantities of Aegean wares made in Crete or the mainland, or in some secondary centre of Mycenaean culture, reached Cyprus between the years 1700 and 1400 B.C., covering the archaeological periods M.M. II to L.M. II. These wares are so few in number that their presence in the island means little more than an occasional contact with the Aegean world that indicates little or no organized trade.

(*b*) The earliest kinds of Mycenaean ware, of L.M. III A type, are not uncommon. This means that some kind of regular intercourse was by this time established between the two cultures, either directly or indirectly.

(c) The imports indicated by the wares in (b) are followed almost immediately by the sudden and immense popularity of Mycenaean wares of all sorts. Many of these wares and many of the ceramic types and styles of painting seem to be of local origin. But the clay is similar to that of true mainland Mycenaean wares, except in a few cases.

(d) Imitations of local make which copied and attempted to rival these real Mycenaean wares naturally grew up. These are easily identified.

Now from these facts many important conclusions that concern archaeological method arise. They are as follows :

(i) Imports of pottery in all ages must be restricted to those vessels which will conveniently travel, or alternatively which will conveniently hold some merchandise which can be taken as well as the pots themselves.

(ii) Identity of clay in ceramic found in two widely separate places does not necessarily imply that the one is derived from the other and that one of the two places is the home of this clay : usually the place where the larger quantity occurs is considered as the centre of dispersal. Actually there can be another solution. The mixing of clay for the work of an expert potter (and Mycenaean potters were experts) is a highly specialized job. For very fine pottery very well-cleansed clay is required. Once the method of preparing the clay has been learned the result will be much the same wherever good clay is found. It is only in poor wares, and where the technique is bad, that the clay can be distinguished. Macedonian prehistoric wares are always distinguishable by the presence of mica fragments in the clay. But if a Mycenaean potter had manipulated Macedonian clay it is probable that the mica fragments would have been eliminated.

It is therefore unscientific to assume that identity of clay means that two fabrics showing this identity come from the same clay deposits. A comparison of the best Attic wares of the classical age and the best Mycenaean wares shows a similarity of clay that is hard to distinguish. The differences are of colour rather than texture, not always even of colour, and that is due to differences of firing rather than to differences of mixing. Fine mainland Geometric wares from widely separate areas are usually made of a clay that is identical.

It is thus very unwise to assume that the similarity of clay in the Cypriot Mycenaean pots to that of Mycenaean pots of the mainland justifies belief in the fact that both were made in Greece. It would be wiser to assume the possibility that large bodies of Mycenaean peoples coming from Greece to Cyprus, brought their potters and their ceramic methods with them and so were able to make Cypriot clay do what the clay of the Argolid or Boeotia could also do.

This at least must be held as an alternative possibility.

(iii) The types of Mycenaean vases in Cyprus are rarely different from those of the mainland. But one very popular class is the crater or amphora (usually decorated with chariot-scenes or other pictorial inventions). These vessels are far too large to make convenient objects of bulk trade. Their fragility is considerable. This suggests that they were made where they were wanted, namely in the island. The ' scattered' nature of the design on these and other Mycenaean vases of Cyprus seems peculiar to the island.[1]

(iv) Whatever case M. Gjerstad may bring to convince himself that the chariot-scenes are not peculiar to Cyprus, he will not convince others. The statistics are against him.[2]

(v) We can only safely assume that vases, which are not obviously intended (like Attic black-figure and red-figure vases) to be primarily works of art, are made as objects of export if they serve some practical and utilitarian purpose. A cargo of vases by Attic masters of the sixth or fifth century was obviously a very valuable cargo indeed. But a cargo of vases each of which could have been made and painted in a few moments would have little exchange value unless the vases contained something saleable. Thus there is no

[1] *Cambridge Ancient History*, vol. i, cf. plates, p. 178.
[2] Cyprus and Syria hold the majority. The apparent examples from Mycenae, Tiryns and Nauplia mentioned by Gjerstad (p. 219) are different in style from the Cypriot chariot vases and not comparable. In Rhodes is one fine chariot-crater, published in *C.V.A.*, *Rodi*, II, 4, 5 and two others, one from tomb xxvii at Makri Vounara, one from tomb lix. The former is painted with red lustrous paint of the kind common in Cyprus. The latter is a very large crater. Neither exhibit the precise and compact draughtsmanship seen in the characteristic octopus-vases of Rhodes. The octopus as an element of design is as prevalent in Rhodes as the chariot in Cyprus.

PLATE V

CYPRIOT AMPHORA OF THE MYCENAEAN PERIOD,
SHOWING BULLS IN HERALDIC POSITION
(*Nicosia Museum*)

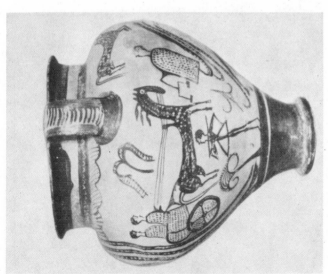

CYPRIOT AMPHORA OF THE MYCENAEAN PERIOD,
OF THE 'CHARIOT SCENE' TYPE
IT SHOWS A CHARIOT, ARMED RETAINER AND
STEWARD WITH SCALES
(*Nicosia Museum*)

reasonable doubt that Corinthian aryballoi, in themselves only very rarely works of art, contained scents and unguents.[1] The same principle applied to Mycenaean pottery rules out the large crater as an article of export (see above) but retains the oenochoe, perhaps the amphora and above all the 'false-necked' vase, the commonest and most widespread of all Mycenaean vessels. The goblet is probably to be ruled out also, because of its extreme fragility, but the askos may be included in the exportable class. But one fact is clear, that wherever Mycenaean ware is found in a setting where it is obviously an import, as at Amarna, Gurob and other Egyptian sites, or in Macedonia,[2] Palestine and Syria, that ware is almost exclusively represented by the 'false-necked' vase, which occurs in a great preponderance. This type of vase was as eminently suited to travel as it was for the retention of liquids or semi-liquids. The larger could have held wines and oils, the smaller unguents. And to prove that these vessels were in fact so used, we have several examples recently published, as acquisitions of a German museum, with their apertures still retaining the seal on the contents, although the contents has presumably evaporated.[3]

While this general rule about export-vases holds for the Mycenaean period, it does not hold for the Middle Minoan Age. The vases of this period, of which

[1] Payne, *Necrocorinthia*, p. 5, n. 3.
[2] In Macedonia there are imported Mycenaean wares and local imitations of them. The same occurs at Troy (see Heurtley, *Quarterly of Palestine Dept. of Antiq.*, vol. V, p. 100).
[3] *Jahrbuch*, 1935, p. 81.

well-known examples of exports, of the Kamares type, have been found in Egypt, are as fragile as they are useless for retaining their contents in transit. They were obviously exported solely as precious works of art and admired for their delicacy of colour and fabric. And such they are, for they were made during the greatest artistic period of Cretan ceramic.

But the implications of the general proposition set out above, must condition all conclusions that concern the import and export of pottery.

We are thus driven to the inference that the very large quantity of Mycenaean wares found in the island was made by Mycenaean peoples who had come into the island and settled, bringing with them their mode of life in all its details—in other words, we arrive inevitably at the conclusion that there was a ' Mycenaean ' colonization of Cyprus somewhere about 1400 or soon after.[1] Myres's date is too early. One must allow for a period during which the Amarna type of pottery took hold as a trade commodity and then was succeeded by a proper influx of Mycenaean peoples.

It remains to verify this conclusion by other means. First it would be obviously advisable to see whether it is possible to identify any special places which might be considered as colonies. If it is found that the distribution of Mycenaean objects is fairly even all over the island, then there would be some reason for accepting the view of ' importation '. But if there appear to be certain specialized areas where Mycen-

---

[1] Cf. Schachermeyer *Hethiter und Achäer*, pp. 103 and 106. This author's acceptance of this date is the most recent statement on the chronology of the Achaean colonization of Cyprus.

aean objects congregate and are, by nature, sufficiently representative of all aspects of the life of a community to justify one in assuming that life in those areas was run on general Mycenaean lines, then the evidence will support the ' colonization ' view.

The facts, as at present known, favour the latter thesis. The great cemeteries of Kurion and Salamis are too comprehensive to let us dismiss them as merely reflecting a Mycenaean influence through the medium of imports. The Larnaka region has equally produced indications of a considerable Mycenaean occupation. They show us a clear picture of Mycenaean life from nearly all aspects, but, as would naturally be expected, with a strong flavour of Cypriot life in it. But the predominant influence is Mycenaean and not Cypriot. The Kurion necropolis was first opened in 1895 by Mr. H. B. Walters, on behalf of the British Museum.[1] Dali (Idalion), Lapethos and Paphos have also revealed typical Mycenaean graves with the usual grave furniture found in the larger cemeteries. Thus five at least of the ancient capitals of kingdoms are seen to go back to the Mycenaean Age—a point of great importance for our study of the political organization of the island (see below, p. 144). It was per-

[1] Myres, *Cyprus Catalogue*, p. 7, and *Cesnola Catalogue*, p. xxx, where he says ' the magnificent tombs of Salamis and Kurion illustrate the prosperity and artistic wealth of Cyprus at this time. Similar colonies founded on the Syrian coast rather later became the seat of that Philistine power which harassed the Israelite tribes until the days of Saul and David (1030–970) '. Myres's assumption of Syrian settlements has, since he made this statement in 1914, been proved right and more fully illustrated by the finds at Ras Shamra.

5

haps at the larger centres like Kurion and Salamis that
the local school of calligraphic vase-painting, represented by the chariot- and bull-craters, grew up.[1]

The general nature of the contents of the Mycenaean tombs of the larger cemeteries shows us a population equipped with most of the furniture of daily
life found in any Mycenaean settlement of mainland
Greece. The shapes and decoration of the smaller
and less ornamental Mycenaean vases is indistinguishable from that on mainland specimens. But local
variations occur, even in fabrics which are entirely
similar to those of the mainland, just as they do at
Rhodes.[2] That is to say, Mycenaean fabrics have
been unconsciously affected in Cyprus by certain
Cypriot shapes. Where these fabrics are indistinguishable from mainland wares technically, this fact
of Cypriot influence would seem decisively in favour
òf our hypothesis that Mycenaean potters actually
worked in the island.

But pottery is not everything. With it were found
typical Mycenaean weapons associated with equally
typical Cypriot weapons showing precisely the kind
of blend of peoples indicated, for instance, in the
earlier Etruscan tombs, where native Villanovan types
occur side by side with intrusive Etruscan.[3] Faience
vases and ornaments of the Egyptianizing and Middle

[1] Myres, *Cyprus Catalogue*, p. 40.

[2] See W. A. Heurtley, *Quarterly of the Dept. of Ant. Palestine*,
V, 3, p. 90 ff. Some unusual types of Mycenaean ware found at
Hissarlik, are also unlike mainland wares (Schmidt, *Schliemann
Sammlung*, Nos. 3563, 3405, 3406) : they seem to me to be
classifiable as Rhodian types.

[3] MacIver : *Villanovans and Early Etruscans*, p. 40 ff.

Eastern types familiar at Mycenae itself are particularly common in Cyprus, especially at Enkomi, so much so that there are logical grounds for thinking that the mainland examples are imports from Cyprus, rather than the reverse. That a special type of faience head-vases and spouted cups was made in Cyprus and from there exported both to Shamra and Assur is certain.[1] They are dated to the period 1300–1250 B.C.

Mycenaean metal-work is also rich and unusual. Bronze tripods, either domestic or ecclesiastical in use, are among the finest examples of Mycenaean metal-work. Two in the Cesnola Collection are of particular merit ; they differ in no detail from similar tripods found in Crete and the mainland.[2] Another fine example is in the Cyprus Museum, and in addition are two finely ornamented cauldron rims, one in the Cesnola Collection,[3] the other in the Cyprus Museum.[4] There are, further, two rectangular bronze cauldron stands which can rank as among the most remarkable Mycenaean bronzes known. One comes from Larnaka and is in the Berlin Museum : the other comes from Enkomi and is in the British Museum.[5] The first is almost intact, a square box, decorated with heraldically facing sphinxes in a rope-pattern border in each panel, surmounted by a circular cauldron

[1] Schachermeyer, pp. 104 and 110. See also Evans, *P. of M.*, IV, ii, p. 771, and Hall, *J.H.S.*, XLVIII, p. 64.

[2] *Cesnola Catalogue*, Nos. 4704 and 4705. Both these belong to about 1200 B.C.

[3] No. 4703. There dated by Myres to 1300–1200 B.C. But Myres would now, he informs me, date it considerably earlier.

[4] Markides, *B.S.A.*, 1913, p. 94.

[5] W. Lamb, *Bronzes*, Pl. XII.

decorated with rope-pattern designs. The whole
rectangular stand is supported by four legs which are
fitted with wheels. It suggests comparison with the
description of the tripods of Hephaestus mentioned
in the XVIII book of the *Iliad* (line 375), which
moved on wheels. The Larnaka example is perhaps
the most elaborate piece of Mycenaean metal-work in
existence, the sphinxes in relief being outstanding as
works of art. The Enkomi example, in a very poor
state of preservation, is equally remarkable in that it
shows in the side-panels women looking out of
windows, rather in the manner of the Palace frescoes
at Knossos. The Enkomi example, indeed, is as
Minoan in character as the Larnaka cauldron is Hittite.
The sphinxes on the panels of the latter bear a close
stylistic relationship with sphinxes on reliefs at Car-
chemish, of the eleventh century B.C. There were undoubtedly throughout Cypriot art of the Mycenaean
period two strains running concurrently—the Minoan,.
which survived in memory, and the Hittite which
came in by the medium of contacts across the straits to
Asia Minor. A third bronze stand comes from Kurion.
It is dealt with below (see Pl. VIII and p. 128).

Bracelets of bronze and gold, ivory boxes, earrings
of gold and various other ornaments all show the
wealth and comfort of Mycenaean Cyprus and illustrate
how it had by this period become wholly westernized.

It is not thus merely a case of occasional imports.
It is rather the absorption by the island of a whole
culture and mode of life.

But there remain other methods of approaching the
problem. Once granted that the main elements of

a material culture had come over *en bloc* to the island,
are there other arguments which suggest that it was
due to the arrival of colonists rather than to the
permeation of trade ?

To this question there are three answers.

Firstly, there survive, scattered in various historical
sources, a large number of records and legends which
all point to one conclusion—the arrival of mainlanders
from Greece in the island as colonists in a remote and
legendary age which in each case seems to be that of
the Achaean predominance of the Homeric or just
pre-Homeric period.   These will be dealt with in a
later chapter (see below, p. 117ff.), but for the moment
it suffices to mention that Kurion was said to be an
Argive colony,[1] that Paphos was ruled by the Cinyrad
dynasty known to Homer, that Idalion possessed a
cult of Apollo Amyklaios, one of the oldest Achaean
cults, and that Lapethos was said by Strabo[2] to be a
Lacedaemonian foundation ; and that on the north
coast there was a place or region known as Ἀχαιῶν
ἀκτή.[3] Keryneia was reputed to be an Achaean
foundation and its name is also found in Achaea.
Golgoi was founded by Sikyonians and a town called
Asine was founded by a colony of Dryopians.   The
bulk of evidence, in short, all points to a general
belief in antiquity that mainland Greeks, chiefly
from the Peloponnese, had come over and colonized
Cyprus.

Secondly, there is the fact, for which Cyprus is
always famous, that with the Mycenaean influx
(whether of goods or of men) came the knowledge

[1] Hdt., v, 113. [2] XIV. 6. 3. [3] See Evans, *Scripta Minoa*, p. 73, n. 3.

of writing. A form of the Minoan script was introduced almost as soon as the first Mycenaean objects were made or imported. The script itself is so important, both in itself and in its bearing on future research, that I have more fully discussed it in a separate chapter (see below, p. 72). But that it was a script known and used by everyday people is apparent from the manner of its occurrence. No actual inscribed tablets, similar to those of Crete, have been found in the island. They may yet be found and their absence from the archaeological collections may be solely due to the fact that hardly any habitation-sites and no palace of the Mycenaean period have yet been excavated in the island. Tombs are not the usual receptacles for tablets and no tablets have been found in Greece or Crete in tombs. There is therefore no probability that they will never be found in the island ; on the contrary, the fact that so many examples of the script have been found inscribed on everyday articles of use almost presupposes that one day more formal records will be found.

Thirdly, there is the extremely significant evidence of the dialect of Greek spoken in classical Cyprus, as illustrated in Cypriot inscriptions, whether in Greek or in the Cypriot script. It belongs to a group which includes both Pamphylian from the Asiatic mainland opposite Cyprus, and Arcadian from the Peloponnese. In the Homeric poems many of the forms used have been shown to be identical with those found in classical Arcadian, and cognate with classical Cypriot.[1] The

[1] C. M. Bowra : ‘Homeric words in Arcadian inscriptions’ in *Class. Quarterly*, 1926, p. 173.

affinity of Cypriot and Arcadian, and of both with Pamphylian forms thus indicates that all alike are derived from a common dialect. It is impossible to presume any intercourse between Arcadia and Cyprus of any importance during the Dark Ages, when the disturbances due to the Dorian movements had effectively cut off Cyprus from the Peloponnese. The causes of the linguistic affinity between Cyprus and mainland Greece must thus go back to pre-Dorian times, before any historic settlement of the island. Taken in conjunction with the foundation legends and the introduction of mainland culture of the Bronze Age type seen in the Peloponnese, the hypothesis of an extensive colonization by a people speaking pre-Dorian Greek who came from mainland Greece is very greatly reinforced. The linguistic evidence alone is insufficient to indicate the date of their arrival.

That the Cypriot script used in the Bronze Age, the Minoan affinities of which are indisputable, was used, when first introduced, as a vehicle for the Greek language, is uncertain.[1] But that it was later used for Greek is beyond dispute. When it was first used for the writing of Greek is a problem for which at present there is no solution. All we know is that a coloniza-

[1] Myres : *Who were the Greeks ?* p. 95, who thinks that the script was introduced by ' people speaking the Minoan language '. Unfortunately we do not yet know whether the people who used the Bronze Age script of mainland Greece used it for Greek or for Minoan. Since, as I have shown in this book, the Cypriot script is allied to that of mainland Greece rather than to that of Crete, we cannot be certain that it was introduced by a Minoan-speaking people until we know that the mainland script was a vehicle for Minoan.

tion of the island appears to have taken place in the late
fifteenth or early fourteenth century, and that with
that colonization came a knowledge of writing in a
medium similar to that of mainland Greece—the mainland version of the Minoan script. The colonists
may have spoken pre-Dorian Greek and written in
Minoan. But they may equally have used their script
both for Minoan and for Greek. Further research in
Cyprus alone can elucidate this point.

The script, as we have it in Cyprus, survives only
in very short inscriptions, almost exclusively on the
sides and handles of vases and jars of clay. The ex-
ceptions are cylinder seals, apparently of local fabric,
inscribed with brief and never very clear inscriptions
in the characters already recognized on the vases and
jars. Also exceptional are three clay balls from
Enkomi, near Salamis, on which inscriptions are
slightly longer than those on the vases and jars. There
is 'also the difference that while all known inscriptions
(apart from one rare group) on vases and jars are
incised, those on the Enkomi balls are impressed on
the clay when it was wet. There is also a group
of vessels which bear signs in paint (see below,
p. 79).

Speaking broadly—and the evidence is at present
too slight to allow definite conclusions—it would
seem that the incised inscriptions on vases and jars are
mainly indications of ownership, mostly cut, as on
woodwork, with a knife after the jar has been fired
and finished. The inscriptions on the Enkomi balls,
on the other hand, point to a knowledge of a cursive
mode of writing exactly similar to that in use on the

Cretan tablets. The painted signs, which are on the underside of the bases of true Mycenaean fabrics, are perhaps in the nature of makers' trade-marks or symbols of manufacture.

The seal-signs, on the other hand, may be names of owners or of gods.

The whole corpus of signs, small though it is, proves conclusively that here in Cyprus something more than a mere assorted collection of imported oddments came into the island. The knowledge of writing took such root in the island that, as is well enough known, it was perpetuated in the historical period down to the end of the fourth century B.C. and respected as something peculiarly Cypriot, and particularly national in quality. A mere trade connexion is not enough to provide so thorough an adoption of an alien custom.

But it must not be forgotten that many elements of Mycenaean life did not reach Cyprus at all, as far as present research can illustrate.[1] The tholos-tomb is unknown in the island. Cyclopean walls and Mycenaean roads or bridges do not occur. In fact, Mycenaean architecture was one of the contributions apparently not acceptable to the islanders or wanted by the colonists. So to a large extent with the religious practices of the Cypriots. There is little trace of Mycenaean religion in Cyprus. The small votive

[1] This is emphatically pointed out by Schachermeyer, who notes that in Cyprus the native Cypriot tomb-type is universal even for full Mycenaean interments, while in Rhodes, at Colophon and Miletus, mainland types of Mycenaean tomb appear. *Hethiter u. Achäer*, p. 98 ff.

figures, so common a feature on mainland sites, are very rare indeed in Cyprus. No sanctuary of the period has been found and there are hardly any Mycenaean objects which illustrate cults and religious practices, such as are seen to such advantage on the gold rings and frescoes of Crete and the mainland.

Another strange lacuna is found in the case of the typical lentoid sealstones, which are so common a feature of all Mycenaean sites on the mainland and in Crete. Hardly any are known in Cyprus. Two only are recorded in the *Catalogue of the Cyprus Museum*[1] and no instance is in the Cesnola Collection —where their rarity is noted in the catalogue.[2] The absence of these seals is probably due to the influence of Babylonia, from whom the Cypriots seem in the Bronze Age to have derived their taste in seals. The obviously Cypriot seals, of homely and uncertain skill, are always cylindrical. This generalization rests on a sound basis, for the number of tombs containing sealstones is considerable, and had Mycenaean seals been popular more would certainly have been found. It is not a deduction based on negative evidence.

Here, then, are several different lines of approach which all lead to the firm conclusion that a powerful process of colonization was set in movement from west to east soon after 1400. The conclusion is reinforced by the mass of evidence from Hittite sources (see below, p. 115) which refer, almost specifically, to Achaean peoples based on Cyprus, and also

[1] p. 32. One in the Ohnefalsch-Richter Collection and one in the British Museum.
[2] p. 410.

by the recent discoveries on the north Syrian coast
of a Levantine port of the Bronze Age at Ras Shamra,
where Mycenaean modes of life were thoroughly at
home. Cyprus thus falls into place as one of various
places in the Levant to which Achaean enterprise
penetrated in the form of movements of people,
expeditions, and exploratory enterprises—the east-
ward push for conquest or wealth, or both, of the
mainland peoples of Greece. The 'importation'
theory, as adequate to explain the Mycenaean character of Cypriot life in the later Bronze Age, is totally
untenable, unless one is prepared to take a purely
parochial and insular view of Cypriot archaeology
and ignore the strength of external and historical
records, as well as of external archaeological research.
To the Achaeans of the Bronze Age from Greece,
Cyprus was a base for further enterprises of wide
extent, and a goal in itself as well. Into the same
category falls the island of Rhodes, equally power-
fully controlled by Mycenaean culture at the same
time. But the exact position of Rhodes in these
Achaean movements is obscure. All we can say with
certainty is that it, like Cyprus, was a secondary centre
of Mycenaean development in the Aegean and Levant,
and that like Cyprus, it has its own idiosyncrasies in
style and manner in its Mycenaean fabrics, but that,
unlike Cyprus, it had fewer insular characteristics and
less power of absorption and survival. Seldom can
we use the term 'Rhodian' as we do 'Cypriot' to
indicate a turn of style and a twist of manner, which
marks all Cypriot productions for so long a space of
time ; there is no 'Ρόδιος χαρακτήρ similar to the

Κύπριος χαρακτήρ, except perhaps in the seventh and
sixth centuries B.C. And there is no example yet
found of the knowledge of a script in Rhodes. Each
island reacted to Mycenaean influences in a different
way. Cyprus definitely made a Mycenaean culture
of its own, in which the Mycenaean elements almost
overpowered the Cypriot. But as the Mycenaean
waned the Cypriot increased, and the close of the
Bronze Age shows the reassertion of many typical
Cypriot elements. The histories of the two islands
are not closely parallel at any time despite their
proximity as close neighbours. Rhodes, at the close
of the Bronze Age, was in the full stream of Dorian
advance southwards ; Cyprus escaped it and perpetuated her Mycenaean inheritance longer and more
faithfully. Cypriot survivals, even those which last
down to to-day, are largely due to this continuity of
insular life, less devastated as it was by the devastations
that accompanied the arrival of the Iron Age in the rest
of the Greek world. Between Rhodes and Cyprus
was an invisible barrier which shut off the violence
of the Aegean. Cyprus withdrew into herself, and
life during this transitional age was dull and poverty-
stricken, unenterprising and dim, but it was continuous
despite the disturbance of life which inevitably resulted
from the Aegean catastrophe.

Among the survivals which were inherited from
this period must almost certainly be placed the Cypriot
kingship. For its existence in Mycenaean times there
is naturally no convincing circumstantial evidence
from archaeological sources ; but it is worth noting

PLATE VI

AGATE SCEPTRE OF THE BRONZE AGE
(Cesnola Collection : New York)

the unusual sceptre made in three parts, of brown and yellow banded agate, said by Cesnola to come from Kurion.   It has no parallel in Greece and belongs to the Bronze Age [1] (Plate VI).   The sceptre is a six-lobed knob with a tubular socket of agate above and below the knob.   In the sockets are traces of an iron shaft.   The metal, at that date a great rarity used for ornament only, would rightly belong to a royal staff of office.   Iron similarly employed in this ceremonial and artistic fashion is found in the tomb of Tutan-khamon, where an iron dagger with an iron blade, two massive amulets and sixteen miniature chisels were found.[2]

A surprisingly close, if not exact, parallel to this agate sceptre has been found in the course of the Swedish excavations at Amathus.   In tomb No. 5, of Early Iron Age date, was found a bronze sceptre measuring 9.4 cm. in height, with a ringed tubular socket, identical with that of the agate sceptre in design, and with a six-lobed head of the same type and pro-portions.   This tomb is dated by the excavators by a scarab found in it to the period of XIXth–XXIInd Dynasty ; this gives a loose date to the Transitional period of the Early Iron Age which is confirmed and made more precise by the pottery.   Amathus has

[1] Myres, *Cesnola Catalogue*, No. 3001, p. 374.   Cesnola, *Cyprus*, p. 309.   That it comes from Kurion is possible, but that it belongs to the dubious 'Treasure of Curium' is another matter. On this last see Myres, *Cesnola Cat.*, Introduction, p. xvi, and also see Vayson de Pradennes, *Les Fraudes en Archéologie Préhis-torique*, p. 492.

[2] The most convenient account of these is to be found in Wain-wright's article in *Antiquity*, 1936, p. 18, 'The coming of Iron '.

produced as yet nothing at all of Mycenaean date, and the sceptre can be considered, therefore, as the sole link with the Mycenaean Age at this town, for it perpetuates a Mycenaean type.

This agate sceptre may be compared with the superb gold enamelled sceptre from near Kurion (see below, p. 156 and Pl. XI) which must belong to the insignia of the Kurion kingship of the early archaic period. Sceptres were also used on the mainland, and Homer's description of the sceptre of Agamemnon and its long history, give us proof enough that Achaean princes bore sceptres ; but no example has been as yet found at any mainland Mycenaean site. The nearest parallel is the regalia of the Minoan priest-king of Mallia, consisting of a ceremonial sword of unusual type and size, with a crystal head, a decorative stone axe carved into the shape of a panther, and other objects.[1] One may also compare the four great Trojan polished axes, three of green nephrite and one of *lapis lazuli*, from Troy II, which must certainly be the regalia of a Trojan king.[2] Semi-precious stones, the crystal of the Mallia sword, the material of which the Trojan axes are made and the agate of which this sceptre is made, all suggest that regalia in the Bronze Age were partly or wholly made of stones which then, as in classical Greece, possessed merits and values of supernatural importance. Indeed, it was probably in the Bronze Age that these stones were first endowed with those qualities which many of them are still to-day said to possess. One would naturally expect to find

[1] *Fouilles executées a Mallia*, Premier rapport, Pl. I, and XXXII.
[2] *Antiquity*, 1933, p. 337.

stones to which magical qualities attached used for royal regalia.[1]

The further fact that five of the cities which were later known capitals of Cypriot local kingdoms contained Mycenaean settlements in the Bronze Age, and that two of these, Kurion and Salamis, were clearly large and thriving Mycenaean colonies, strongly suggests that the immigrant colonists of the Mycenaean world, who substantially were of mainland stock, had brought with them one of the most striking features of the Achaean world of the Mainland, the Achaean kingship. This kingship, which will be dealt with more fully below (see p. 144 ff.), was a semi-democratic constitutional monarchy of the type so fully illustrated in Homer. The king was no despot and had to refer his control periodically to the agreement of his people. But at the same time it was a semi-divine monarchy. It is much more likely that the Cypriot kingship derives from the Achaean mainland prototype than from the Minoan priest-kingship, if only for the fact that, while the presence of Achaean colonists is amply attested in the island, there is no certain evidence that Minoans ever reached the island except by way of occasional trade, and that too is problematical, for all the Minoan contacts may equally be explained by indirect trade through Egypt.

[1] The value attached to agate in antiquity varied : one type, known as λεοντοδερής, is described in the Orphika (*Lith*: 613) τῷ καί μιν προτέροισι λεοντοδέρην ὀνομῆναι, ἥνδανεν ἡμιθέοισι. The agate of which the sceptre in the Cesnola Collection is made is yellow and brown and so may be classed as of the type λεοντοδερής. The fact that demigods favoured it in ' early times ' strengthens our classification of this object as regalia.

The complete absence of Mycenaean remains on the actual sites of Amathus,[1] Kition[2] and Soloi, may or may not be significant. To draw conclusions from this negative evidence would be unwise. But it is perhaps worth noting that no legend of foundation referring to mainland Greece occurs in either case, that Kition was generally believed to be a Phoenician foundation, so post-dating the Bronze Age, and that Amathus followed a pro-Persian politic in the struggle with Persia. Amathus was reputed to be one of the oldest cities in the island, which makes it all the more strange that it had no mainland foundation-legend. Possibly we may infer from this that it was a native Cypriot city and untouched by the Achaean colonization.[3] It is significant that the inscription (in two parts) in the Ashmolean Museum in the Cypriot Syllabary of the historic period was found at Limassol near Amathus. This inscription is in an unknown language. But the absence of Mycenaean remains at

[1] Hill, B.M. Catalogue of Coins, p. xxiv ; B.M. Excavations in Cyprus, p. 89. Recently confirmed anew by the Swedish excavators who after excavating twenty-six more tombs state that 'no Late Cypriot pottery has ever been found at Amathus'. Gjerstad, S.C.E., 1935, II, p. 2.

[2] Mycenaean remains are plentiful near Larnaka and in Prof. Myres's excavations in 1913 (unpublished) at Bamboula sub-Mycenaean pottery was found at the lowest level.

[3] This is strongly borne out by the fact that Scylax Caryandensis in his all too brief note on Cyprus (Ch. 103) states that it is a city of the αὐτόχθονες in contrast with cities of the Greeks and of the Phoenicians. Stephanus of Byzantium states that it is the oldest city of the island. He also states (s.v. Kypros) that another name for Cyprus was Amathousia. But the name Amathus is Greek, descriptive of the sandy coast. No pre-Greek name survives.

these three places accords with their history as we know it. If Mycenaean objects are, in fact, found at them, then it will be necessary to revise these suggestions.

The close of the Bronze Age brings Cyprus into the orbit of an immense and catastrophic upheaval of the ancient world. By 1100 B.C. at latest the Hittite power of Anatolia had fallen already before invading hordes of European peoples who swept across almost to the Syrian border, Moschoi, Phrygians and other allied peoples constantly referred to in Greek and Assyrian records.[1] Troy also fell to one wave of this inrush. The last city of the Bronze Age was occupied after destruction by a people who came from Central Europe, a branch of the great Lausitz movement.[2] Israelite kings destroyed the Philistine hold on the coast, which reverted now to full Semitic control. Egypt withdrew into herself and watched affairs in an almost American isolation from entanglements, and beat off by superior organization all attempts at raids on her Delta. But she abandoned her northern frontier in Palestine. In 1194 Ramses III had successfully held up a northern invasion in Philistia, but later the Egyptian Empire was withdrawn. It was on the occasion of this victory in the Palestine coastlands that we get a list of hostile cities mentioned by Ramses [3] which are by some identified as Cypriot cities—Salamis, Kition, Idalion and Soloi, the inference being that Cypriots as well as others were pushing eastwards.

Cyprus, however, escaped the force of these inroads

[1] A. R. Burn, *Minoans, Philistines and Greeks*, p. 141 ff.
[2] V. G. Childe, *The Danube in Prehistory*, p. 416.
[3] Oberhummer, p. 4.

into Asia Minor and stood equally clear of the sea-
movements which engulfed her neighbour Rhodes
and brought to Rhodes that solid settlement of Dorians
which made Rhodes throughout antiquity a powerful
Dorian settlement.   Cyprus drifted almost unconsciously into an Iron Age.   While in mainland Greece
every city went up in flames and even villages were
sacked, Cyprus carried her Mycenaean traditions and
manners of life into a new era.   But it was an era of
poverty and decline, and Cyprus no less than Greece
itself passes through a long and tedious Dark Age in
which little stirred either of culture or prosperity.
Cypriot life, however, was carried on in the traditional Cypriot manner.   Again her power for survival
asserted itself.   Among the survivals that lasted from
the Bronze Age and were perpetuated into Classical
Cyprus were the two most important inheritances
from the Achaean Age—the kingship and the knowledge of writing.   At least I propose that hypothesis,
allowing for reasonable doubts in the case of the
former but postulating certainty in the latter.   The
kingship *may* be post-Achaean, but the survival of the
Cypriot script down to Hellenistic times is universally
accepted as due to the fact that it is a development of
the Bronze Age script brought over from the Aegean
in the full Bronze Age of the Achaean colonization.

Myres sees, at the close of the Cypriot Bronze Age,
a more violent interruption of life than I have here
presupposed. ' Very shortly after the reign of Ramses
II,' he says, ' this Minoan civilization of Cyprus came
to an abrupt and violent end.'[1]   Burial sites are

[1] Myres, *Who were the Greeks?* p. 128.

changed. The Mycenaean Salamis and, at Kition, the lake-side settlement is abandoned for one on the shore. But the disturbance was not universal, as the site of Aghios Jakovos shows (see below, p. 141) and the fact that it is coastal towns that illustrate the disturbance suggests that they were sacked from the sea rather than by any large intrusion into the island. Probably they were attacked by roaming pirates.

The approach of a new age is heralded by the gradual restriction of skill, invention and imagination on the part of the island artists. A dull repetition creeps into their ceramic and a poorness of technique is visible both in their shapes, their clay and the paint that adorned all vases. No longer was fresh inspiration coming over from the mainland. We see the old designs resifted, juggled with again and reused *ad nauseam*. Hard geometrical ornament takes the place of the happier curves of the finer and earlier wares, and a steady degradation of floral and marine devices ensues. Much the same was happening in mainland Greece and Crete now that communications were restricted and poverty increasing. Vases revert for inspiration to pre-Mycenaean shapes and patterns [1] or look to animal-shapes, to metal-work and to basket wares for inspiration. The natural playfulness of the Cypriot potter of the Early Bronze Age, when he experimented in strange shapes and complicated clay virtuosities, is emerging as the foreign tutelage is weakening.

[1] *Cesnola Catalogue*, Nos. 400–411, where the potter is searching in new directions for ideas. The general character still remains Mycenaean, but the wares are no longer to be confused with genuine mainland productions. The native Cypriot is asserting himself once more.

CHAPTER III

THE CYPRIOT SCRIPT

THE fact that a method of writing was in use in Cyprus in the Bronze Age was recognized as soon as the cemeteries of the Bronze Age were fully and adequately excavated. Previously, as early as 1852 it had been realized that in Classical times a mode of writing Greek other than in Greek letters had existed in the island, a fact unique in the Greek world.[1] But it was not until well after 1880 that scholars began gradually to realize, as evidence accumulated, that a Bronze Age script had also been in existence. Cesnola in his publication of *Cyprus* in 1878, gave no indication that he had identified any writing of the pre-Classical period, though he discussed fully, and with some scholarship, the known classical script. Sayce, however, in 1905 pointed out that certain signs on a cylinder found in a cemetery at Aghia Paraskeve indicated that the Cypriot script is thus not confined to the Classical Age but ' taken back to an age contemporaneous with the Kretan linear characters ' ;[2]

[1] By the Duc de Luynes in his publication, *Numismatique et Inscriptions Cypriotes*, issued in that year.

[2] *Proc. Soc. Bibl. Arch.*, xxvii, p. 254 and Pl. xi. Evans, *Palace of Minos*, IV, ii, p. 763. Ward, *Seal-cylinders of Western Asia*, p. 345. The cylinder is in the Ashmolean Museum.

and Evans in 1911 at last elaborated the thesis previously suggested by him in 1899 that there was a fully established Cypriot script in use in the Bronze Age which bore some affinity to the Cretan script.[1] Again in 1935 Evans has amplified his study of the Cypriot script.[2] He repeats with greater emphasis the belief that the script is closely dependent upon, if not actually derivative from, the Cretan Linear A and B scripts. But he notes certain important points. Thus :

(1) Mainland Greek versions of the advanced linear Cretan scripts (with which he has most fully dealt in the volume referred to) contain certain signs, apparently peculiar to the mainland. Not a single one of these signs is found in the Cypriot series. (This is, however, not the case ; see below, p. 89.)

(2) He disagrees with Sayce in thinking that the Aghia Paraskeve cylinder above referred to is illustrative of the Cypriot script proper. He had already adumbrated this view in *Scripta Minoa*. He thinks that its Early Bronze Age (or ' Copper Age ') date is certain and that in consequence it indicates a knowledge of writing in Cyprus earlier than the Cretan connexion. In his opinion it ' indicates an independent tradition of early script, going back centuries before the date of the Minoan plantations ' on the island.

Evans notes that ' in number, the published examples of the Bronze Age script of Cyprus are very limited ',[3] so that his generalizations are naturally rather reserved

[1] *J.R.A.I.*, xxx, p. 217. *Scripta Minoa I*, p. 71 ff.
[2] *P. of M.*, IV, ii, p. 758 ff.
[3] Ibid., p. 758.

and restricted.   The actual number of signs published
in *Scripta Minoa* was fifteen and in the *Palace of Minos*
he discusses others from an incised inscription on a
vase fragment,[1] from Enkomi.   The fifteen signs published in *Scripta Minoa* are made up from inscriptions
on a gold ring from Larnaka, and on three clay balls
from Enkomi.   The material was thus not large.   In
the *Palace of Minos* one further Enkomi ball is published, and in all still fifteen signs only are given,
though there are some changes in the new list.[2]   In
1932 Persson published the three balls shown by Evans
in the *Palace of Minos*, with the one published in *Scripta
Minoa* and omitted from the later publication [3] and
adds a fifth [4] not previously published.

Of these clay objects four are clearly legible.   But
one [5] bears signs which are so small and uncertain that

---

[1] *P. of M.*, IV, ii, p. 759, Fig. 741.   Evans wrongly describes it
as on a ' limestone fragment ' and states that it comes from the
' Minoan akropolis '.   It was found in the necropolis of Enkomi.
See Myres, *Man.*, 26, 1934, where it is stated to be ceramic.
Evans's interpretation of the last sign on the right as a double-axe
is untenable.   The photographs in *Man* do not support his transcription.   The sign in question is, in fact, identical with another,
also incised on a vase, published by Markides.   It falls into line
with a group of Cypriot signs in which the triangle is a predominant element (see below).   The sign is ⚡ (No. 7 below,
p. 99).

[2] Thus the new list omits sign 13 (on the Larnaka ring) as
well as signs 7 and 8 of *Scripta Minoa* and replaces them by
three new signs (Nos. 8, 13 and 14).

[3] *Scripta Minoa*, Fig. 37 (middle inscription) = Persson's inscription C.   A. W. Persson, *Symbola Philologica*, p. 269.

[4] His inscription E.

[5] Which Evans omitted from *P. of M.*

it must be ruled out as likely to contribute many signs which can be transcribed reliably. Persson publishes it without a transcription.

Here, then, is the slender corpus of material up to the date of Evans's most recent consideration of the problem. Five clay balls, inscribed with a stylus or some similar instrument when the clay was wet, one gold ring and one inscription cut with a knife on baked pottery. That is not much, and certainly not enough to allow of more than the most tenuous research into the problem of Bronze Age writing in Cyprus. And yet Evans, commenting on the obvious relationship of some of his signs with those of the Classical script, remarks that

the old syllabic script had been (in Classical times) very imperfectly adapted as a vehicle for Greek writing in an age when, outside this conservative island, the Semitic alphabet had been generally adopted. This persistence, beside the very cradle of writing of the more imperfect local tradition is itself one of the strangest phenomena in the History of Writing. . . . With these (characters) rests the only real hope of even approximately learning the values of the Minoan signs (*P. of M.*, IV, ii, p. 761).

There survives, however, much more material for the study of the Cypriot script than that with which Evans and Persson deal. As will be seen later, it is possible now to accumulate a much larger total of signs of the Bronze Age script. It is also possible to get some general idea as to the character of the Cypriot script and of the relative frequency of signs. Once relative frequency is established—and only a fairly large corpus of material can make this possible —we have at least one clue to decipherment, or at least a clue which can be held in reserve. But in dealing with the Cypriot script in itself we have the enormous advantage from the point of view of decipherment, of knowing that many of the signs of the Bronze Age are exactly paralleled by signs of the Classical Age of which we know the sound-values. The new material here collected now makes it possible to establish the equation of the prehistoric and the historic scripts much more closely. It is no part of the purpose of this book even to attempt to proceed further to solve any of the problems of the Minoan scripts, but it may serve others to state plainly the ascertained facts and to show to what extent the Cypriot sign-groups can be transformed into sound and into legible words. Even so, we do not yet know what language the Bronze Age Cypriots spoke, whether they spoke one language only and whether either or any of the languages they spoke was Minoan. It is thus better at this stage to set forth the evidence and state the facts and leave the larger enterprise to others. From the facts we can at least formulate conclusions of great value for a study of the literacy of the Bronze Age Cypriots and for an examination of the growth of a mode of writing.

I shall not here presuppose any connexion between the prehistoric and the Classical Cypriot scripts, even though that presupposition is almost universally recognized by scholars and is probable from a study of the facts here presented. But I shall leave the connexion to make itself evident or otherwise as the analysis proceeds.

The material for study can be classified as follows :

Class I.

Signs, clearly and distinctly made are found on vases. The vases on which these signs occur are (i) painted vases of the Mycenaean of Cypro-Mycenaean types and (ii) plain vessels of ordinary domestic types, usually jars and amphorae of whitish-yellow ware, and (iii) undecorated vases of the Bronze Age wheel-made red ware (Fabric VII of the Cesnola Collection). I propose to consider these different classes separately.

(i) This class can be subdivided into two parts :
    a. Painted vases bearing incised signs.
    b. Painted vases bearing painted signs.

The signs incised on painted vases are always incised on the handles through the paint and clearly so inscribed after the vases have been fired.

The signs made in paint on painted vases are all made on the *under side of the bases* of the vessels in a reddish paint corresponding to the paint used for the actual decoration of the vase. It is thus clear that these are two totally different types of inscriptions.

The signs inscribed by incision on painted vases of type *a* are all scratched or cut with a point or knife through a painted or partly painted surface.

Type *a* therefore consists of inscriptions which might have been made by the maker but which also could have been made by the owner.

Type *b* consists of inscriptions which are more likely to have been made by the maker of the vase. This is an important distinction. It is also worth noting that the painted signs are in every case single signs of some size painted always on the under side of the base, with a broad brush ; they are the largest inscriptions which we possess in script in Cyprus, the letters in some cases measuring as much as 10 cm. in height.[1]

No inscriptions of this type have as yet been recorded on vessels of Mycenaean fabric from Mainland Greece. There the painted inscriptions are always on the necks or sides of vessels.[2]

The recorded examples of type (i)*a* are as follows :

1. Cesnola Collection. No. 438. Myres, *Catalogue*, p. 525. Two signs.

2. British Museum. No. C. 379. Large crater (fragmentary). One sign (? possibly two) incised on handle. From Maroni.

3. British Museum. C. 430. Three-handled jar. Two signs, each on a handle. From Enkomi (1896).

4. British Museum. C. 434. Three-handled jar. Two signs, each on a handle. From near the Salt Lake, Larnaka.

5. British Museum. False-necked jar, C. 501, with two handles. On each handle is incised the same sign. From excavations at Kurion.

6. British Museum. C. 523. False-necked jar. Two signs, each on a handle. Enkomi, excavations of 1896.

7–10. British Museum. Four signs (unpublished).

Here, then, are no less than twelve incised signs. One is repeated twice, otherwise all the signs are different.

[1] As in No. 8 of our table below on p. 99.
[2] Evans, *P. of M*, IV, ii, p. 740 ff. Three mainland examples are given by Professor Schaeffer in *Missions en Chypre*, Appendix I, nos. xxvi–xxviii. But they seem to me to be mere haphazard designs and neither Minoan nor Cypriot signs of recognizable types.

The recorded examples of type (1)*b* are of unusual interest. I have collected eight examples of Mycenean vases found in Cyprus with signs clearly painted on the base and can now add to the list further examples found by Professor C. Schaeffer, who has kindly allowed me access to his material. The total of authentic examples from Cyprus now amounts to nineteen. Professor Schaeffer and I discovered that we were working on this type at the same time. He has published his account of the painted signs in a recent article (Feb. 1937) in *Missions en Chypre*, Appendix I. The complete series will be found in my list below (p. 98 ff.) where they are correlated with other instances of the signs. Professor Schaeffer, whose study is concerned more with the ceramic than the linguistic aspect of the signs, considers them to be proofs of the manufacture in Cyprus of standard Mycenaean ware in the thirteenth century. I have not dealt here with examples of the painted signs found outside Cyprus except the group from Palestine (see p. 108).

I am in entire agreement with Professor Schaeffer that the signs painted on the vases are trade-marks, peculiar to Cyprus and that they afford proof additional to the other evidence adduced above for the existence of local Cypriot factories of Mycenaean ceramic.

The known or recorded examples of Class I (ii) are far more numerous. I will not catalogue them here, since in the appended final list of signs it is possible to identify each instance. In this class the majority of inscriptions consist, as in type (i)*a*, of single signs inscribed on the handles of jars. But this is not the rule. There are three inscriptions of some length ; indeed they constitute the longest inscriptions in the Bronze Age script yet recorded. They are as follows :

1. A large jug of plain ware of the typical yellow-buff Cypriot domestic ware of the Mycenaean period. On the shoulder are four signs of which the first two look like numerals. See Markides, *Annual Report of the Curator of Antiquities*, Cyprus, 1916, p. 16. From Katydhata.

2. A fragment of a large pithos of rough reddish ware from Arpera bearing six signs in three groups, divided by vertical strokes. The first group consists of three signs, the second of one and the third of two. Markides, op. cit., p. 17, No. 9.

3. A fragment of a large pithos of plain whitish ware bearing five signs inscribed on the body. Markides, op. cit., p. 18, No. 11; Evans ; *P. of M.*, IV. ii, p. 759 ; Myres, *Man*, 26, 1934. (Referred to above, p. 74.)

But, in the main, inscriptions are on handles and consist of single or at most two signs. The signs are always cut with a knife, the knife-cuts being always clear to the eye : they were thus made after firing and so can have been made equally by owner or maker, as in the case of type (i)*a*.

A distinction must be made between the incised signs of type (i)*a* and (ii) and the painted inscriptions of type (i)*b*. The former seem by their nature to be indicative of either ownership or of contents of the vessels. The neck and the shoulder of vessels, being the most prominent parts ordinarily seen when the vessels were in store, or arranged in rows, are the parts inscribed. The particular inscription bearing what seem to be numerals, No. 1 of type (ii) above described seems to bear out the theory that it is the contents which is referred to. The three rather long inscriptions may all belong to this class of inscription, equivalent to the labels on wine bottles. The handle inscriptions, on the other hand, are brief indications, perhaps of ownership, resembling rather the glass stamps of cellarers on eighteenth-century port bottles.

The distribution of the inscribed vessels shows that the knowledge of what these signs indicated was spread over most of the island. That they were found at Enkomi, Katydhata in the Soloi district on the north coast, Larnaka, Maroni, between Larnaka and Amathus, and Kurion, shows that the script was diffused over the entire island, and not a local development in one intensely populated area.

The quantity of the evidence considered in relation to the circumstances in which it occurs justifies us in assuming that the knowledge of writing was diffused throughout the population and not merely the prerogative of priests and princes. Hitherto no indubitably sacred object bearing an inscription has been found.

Type I (iii) of our classification of inscribed vases refers to a wheel-made red ware, the prevailing shapes of which are lentoid flasks, ovoid jugs and spindle-shaped bottles. The type is that of Myres (*Cyprus Catalogue*, I, 8, and *Cesnola Catalogue*, Fabric VII). It may perhaps not be a native Cypriot ware, as it is of frequent occurrence in Palestine.

The following instances of inscribed signs are recorded for this type :

1. British Museum. C. 191 from Klavdia near
   Larnaka, one sign on handle.
2. Myres, *Cesnola Catalogue*, No. 376, p. 41.
3.   „   „   „   No. 377, p. 41.
4.   „   „   „   No. 378, p. 41.
5.   „   „   „   No. 379, p. 41.
6.   „   „   „   No. 381, p. 41.

Myres notes that the signs are ' incised on the clay
before firing, usually at the base or on the handle ';
it is also the case in the British Museum example
No. 1 above.[1]

It remains to consider other main classifications
under which we can accumulate material. Under
Class I, I have grouped all vase inscriptions, painted
or impressed before firing or incised after firing.

Examples of inscriptions made on wet clay are
found in the case of the clay balls from Enkomi. This
therefore forms our Class II. The material, exiguous
though it is, is of extreme importance and consists
of the following :

Class II.

1. An ovoid clay ball. It bears an inscription of
eight signs, all legible, divided into two groups by
vertical strokes. One group consists of three signs,
the other of five.

2. An ovoid clay ball. It bears an inscription consisting of four signs, all legible, divided into two parts,

[1] Another sign incised before firing is shown under No. 16 in
the table. But the fabric is not Fabric VII.

one consisting of one sign, the other of three, the division being indicated by a vertical stroke.

3. An ovoid clay ball. It bears an inscription consisting of six signs of which the last is not clearly legible.

4. An ovoid clay ball. It bears a legible inscription of three signs.

5. An ovoid clay ball. It bears an inscription of seven signs, not divided by vertical strokes at any point. Of these signs two only are clearly legible (the first and fourth in Persson's plate E) and appear to be the same sign.

6. A solitary instance of a sign impressed on a vase (on the handle) when the clay was wet. It comes from Enkomi and is unpublished. It is No. 1593 in the Nicosia Museum. See table below (p. 100), No. 16. The vase is an ordinary plain domestic ware as used in type I (ii) above.

These inscriptions on clay balls have been discussed by Evans and Persson.[1] I cannot here accept Persson's transliteration of the signs on Nos. 1–5 into equivalents of the Classical Cypriot script. A glance at his transcription makes it evident that there is a very wide difference between the original signs and the signs which he selects to equate with them. His transcriptions, together with the consequent translation and interpretation, falls to the ground as a result. Nor am I convinced of his interpretation of the purpose of these balls—that they were weights for the weighing

[1] Evans, loc. cit., and A. W. Persson, ' Some inscribed terracotta balls from Enkomi' published in *Symbola Philologica. O. A. Danielsson octogenario dicata.* Upsala, 1932.

of gold. Evans's alternative interpretation that they are votive objects is more probable, but still unconvincing. The circumstances of the finding of these balls are such that we can draw no valid inferences. It would be better to wait until further examples are found in more scientific conditions before a decision as to their use and purpose is made. It is sufficient to note that they indicate that the Cypriot script could be written on soft material by means of a stylus as well as cut on hard surfaces with a knife. The script on these balls, moreover, follows the methods of writing employed on the vases. Signs are similarly divided into groups by vertical strokes and the signs on the examples of Class II are in several cases repeated in the inscriptions of Class I. Both classes, in short, give the same script at the same stage of linear development. There seems no reason to postulate any difference of date between the two classes.

Into a Class III have been placed all instances of inscriptions which occur on materials other than clay, excluding cylinders and seals, which I have made into Class IV.

Class III.

A copper ingot from Enkomi (see No. 17 in the table) bears a sign of which two other instances are known. Strangely enough there are no inscriptions on stone yet recorded, except for the unreliable examples of masons' marks, found by peasants without any observed archaeological context and published by Markides[1] :

[1] C.A.R., p. 22. Found at Styloi near Famagusta.

these masons' marks are three in number, as follows :

⋈ ⊥ φ

The first, though of Cretan character, does not appear in the assembled instances of known signs (see p. 98 ff.),[1] the second is common both to the prehistoric and the historic script, and the third appears in the historic but not as yet in the prehistoric script. It might also be Greek.

There are also no inscriptions extant in wood or ivory, but there survives one unusual bronze plaque bearing what is apparently the representation of a woman in Minoan or Mycenaean dress milking a goat or cow.[2] The design is made by moulding. The metal seems to have been poured into a mould on which the design was sketched *intaglio*. This mould was probably of clay, for the design has a blurred surface which suggests that the design had been lightly and hastily sketched on the surface of clay with a stylus. In the field above the design are three clear Cypriot signs, all already known. They are the signs ⟰ ╈ and ╞ . The first occurs also on one of the clay balls from Enkomi, the second is common, known in five other cases and the third is known in two other cases (see table below, p. 100–2, Nos. 17, 26 and 27).

---

[1] Evans's identification of this sign on the inscription referred to above, p. 74, n. 1, is not acceptable for reasons there given.

[2] It is in private possession and is said to come from Larnaka. A replica of it is in the Ashmolean Museum.

7

Class IV.

Into this class I have accumulated the exiguous and not very satisfactory evidence of a variety of seals and a ring on which are inscriptions.

The first is the gold ring,[1] found in a tomb excavated by Mr. H. B. Walters near the Tekke, close to Larnaka. On this I prefer to see only three clear signs, which I have incorporated in the table (Nos. 23, 43, 44). Of these three signs one only is common in Bronze Age script and equally common in the Classical. The other two are found only in the Classical script. The fourth sign identified by Evans seems to me to be a part of the decoration and not a sign. The fact that the knowledge of the Bronze Age script which can be gleaned from the details assembled here in the table (p. 98 ff.) shows that the inscription on the ring conforms ill with the Bronze Age script tends to strengthen Dussaud's supposition that it is of the Classical Age,[2] but since Dussaud adduces no evidence to prove this late date and Evans states categorically that it was found in a Bronze Age tomb associated with objects of Late Mycenaean date, I am compelled, until better information is forthcoming, to include it in my evidence. Its three signs are thus shown in the table. The ring, however, cannot rank as a serious contributor to the study of the script in view of its uncertain date.

[1] Evans, *P. of M.*, p. 759 ; *Scripta Minoa*, p. 70. In the later publication Evans has inexplicably omitted one of the signs. As there is no clear reason for this I have retained it in my table. The sign in question is the 8.

[2] *Civilizations Préhelléniques*, p. 431, n. 2.

The second object is a cylinder (see above, p. 72) which Sayce thought to be Mycenaean, which Dussaud considers to be Cypriot contemporary with the inscribed objects of the Late Bronze Age, and which Evans, in his latest expression of view, takes to be pre-Mycenaean Cypriot and an early testimony to a knowledge of writing other than the script in the island. The cylinder was found at Aghia Paraskeve.[1] But a comparison of its transcription in Evans and Dussaud and a comparison of these with the drawing in Ward shows such wide discrepancies that I do not feel assured in drawing from its small group of about five signs. It looks more like a Late Mycenaean seal than one of pre-Mycenaean date, and the device carved on it, inscription apart, seems to belong to the quasi-geometric barbaric stage of seal-carving rather than to the Early Bronze Age.

Two other cylinders are mentioned by Dussaud,[2] one as in the Louvre and one in the Bibliothèque Nationale.[3] Of these one in the Louvre (Fig. 320) bears two signs of which one is our No. 48 (see list on p. 105) and the other not otherwise known. The other example in the Louvre (Fig. 319) has three pictographic signs and one linear. The linear sign is No. 46 in our list. All these are definitely Cypriot linear signs. The example in the Bibliothèque

---

[1] Evans, P. of M., IV., ii, p. 763, Fig. 745 ; Dussaud, op. cit., p. 429 ; Ward, op. cit., No. 1165.

[2] Op. cit., Figs. 319 and 320.

[3] Delaporte, Cat. de cylindres orientaux (Bibl. Nat.), No. 478. This cylinder comes from the collection of the Duc de Luynes and so almost certainly comes from Cyprus.

Nationale has three signs of which one is the sign
No. 46 above. The other two signs are not otherwise known.

Another cylinder to add to this group is No. 4311
in the Cesnola Collection (Ward No. 1164). It
shows clearly five signs of which four are our Nos.
23, 24, 34 and 45. The fifth may be our No. 9.

Of the script as a whole it must be said that the signs
as shown in the table below are almost all of a rectilinear type.[1] The only signs which are an exception
out of a total of forty-seven are Nos. 32, 43 and 44.
The last two come from the Larnaka gold ring, one
of them being a definite Egyptian *ankh* sign. This
again makes it evident how this gold ring is out of
harmony with the other evidence.

The rectilinear nature of the script suggests that it
was invented in the first instance for carving on to a
flat surface. Indeed at first glance it looks as if it were
primarily a wood-carved script, like Ogham, easily
adapted to harder surfaces like pottery or stone. It is
at least certain that all the pottery inscriptions that are
not in paint except one are cut with a knife on the
hard surface of vases after firing. A script so inscribed
would be no less easily adaptable to recording by
means of a stylus on soft clay, and this in fact we
also find.

It seems certain that the script did not evolve from
any previous series of pictographic Cypriot signs, for
there are none. It must thus have been either invented
in the island or brought in from outside in a developed
linear form. Its connexions with the Cretan script

[1] Myres calls attention to this. *Cesnola Catalogue*, p. 301.

are pointed out by Evans, and I do not propose to go
into them here. It suffices in this book to collect all
recorded Cypriot examples. As shown in the table
below, it is remarkable how they agree in type and
form as a homogeneous group.

In the four classes of inscription described above
it is now possible to accumulate a gross total of
109 known signs, from which total, when repetitions
are allowed for, a total signary of sixty-one signs
emerges. In addition there are five other signs which
are probably numerals. We can say, then, that
we have knowledge of at least a total of sixty-six
variant signs. This is an advance on the total of
fifteen published by Evans in 1935.

Evans has stated that no single sign of those peculiar
to the Mainland Greek version of the Minoan script
appears in the Cypriot (see above, p. 73). But his
conclusion was based only on the small group of
Cypriot signs which he has published. A comparison
of the table here printed with the list of Theban signs
published by Evans in the *Palace of Minos* (IV, ii,
p. 740, Fig. 724a and b) shows that many of the
Theban signs, painted on the shoulders of Mycenaean
vessels, appear also in the Cypriot script. Thus our
Nos. 2, 3, 4, 23, 24, 26, 36, 38 and 46, all appear in
the Theban group. In the other group of mainland
signs shown in Fig. 725 we can see our signs Nos, 1,
4, 26, 30 and 45. Nos. 30 and 36 are certainly
identical with signs in the list of eleven shown by
Evans (op. cit., Fig. 735) to be peculiar to the mainland. The general nature of the mainland signs, even
allowing for the fact that they are painted, is largely

rectilinear, but it is true that a certain number of curvilinear signs do appear, which have no parallel at present in the Cypriot series. The comparison shows that the two scripts are certainly connected and a consequent connexion between the mainland of Greece and Cyprus is to be inferred in matters of writing. The fact that the mainland connexions of Cyprus are so fully documented by the purely archaeological evidence gives an added significance to this close relationship of the scripts.

Of this total of sixty-one signs, numerals excluded, the two signs, Nos. 43 and 44, may possibly be of the Classical period, but are here included, until more definite evidence for their dating is found, for at present the indications are that they *may* belong to the Bronze Age.

Out of the total there are seven exact correspondences with the Classical script, namely the signs for Pa, La, Na, Lo, Ta, E and Le, and probable equations in the case of signs which appear to be the same as the Classical signs for Si (either No. 10 or No. 17), for Ra, for Mo and for Vo, a total of four more. Thus there is a correspondence between the prehistoric and the historic scripts that may cover about a sixth of the recorded signs. Whether this may be considered as sufficient to enable us to conclude that the later script is derived from the earlier, I must leave others to judge. Such a conclusion would seem probable on the evidence available.

But the proof must be sought for in that dim period which intervenes between the latest usage of the Bronze Age script and the earliest examples of the

Classical. And this is a most obscure period. The surprising fact is that during the Early Iron Age there is little evidence to show that the knowledge and practice of the script was maintained. It seems to have fallen into desuetude. Although the quantity of Early Iron Age vases and other remains is, perhaps, even larger than that which represents the Late Bronze Age, yet the number of inscribed objects is extremely limited. There survive only the following inscriptions :

a. A sub-Mycenaean jug from Cyprus (exact place unknown). *B.Mus.Cat.*, I. 2, p. 133, No. C. 699, which has the following mark on its shoulder : Ύ

b. A red bucchero oenochoe in the Cesnola Collection, Myres, No. 474, p. 59 and 525, which bears four signs, as follows : ⊍⟨⟨ ⟩ m

c. A red bucchero jug with the following incised inscription ; in the Cesnola Collection, No. 481 :

Ϥ 𝟪 ⊢
se le ta

d. A similar red bucchero jug with the following incised inscription, in the Cesnola Collection, No. 480.

Ϝ 𝖷 Ψ 𝖠 ⟋ Ϝ Ⅴ
ᵖpa ro te ko ta to no

e. A vase of green steatite, No. 1540 in the Cesnola Collection, bearing three linear signs incised on the base on the under side. This vessel is given the tentative date of Late Bronze Age, but it may equally be Early Iron Age. The signs are as follows :

Ħ ⊟ E

This is the total information hitherto recorded for

the transitional period between the Late Bronze Age
and the Early Iron Age and for the Early Iron Age as
a whole. It is disappointing and does not amount to
much. The single sign on *a* might possibly be the
sign No. 15 in our table. But the inscription on *b*
could equally well be an illiterate attempt at primitive
Greek, for I can see no true parallel with the script.
The three signs on *c*, and the seven signs on *d*, on the
other hand, are all identifiable with the signs of the
Classical script, and only partly correspond with those
of the Bronze Age script. Both *c* and *d* have been read
and are given by Myres as ta-le-se, or the proper name
Thales in the first and as te-ro-pa-no-to-ta-ko, which
in Greek is Θηροφάνω τῶ ταγῶ. The enigmatic
vessel *e* bears signs which have been wrongly read
as Phoenician.[1] They seem to correspond with the
signs of our table Nos. 24, 38 and 5, and so to conform
to the early stages of the script in the Bronze Age.

It is thus evident both that the Classical type of
script, as known from the sixth century onwards, was
fully formed by the Early Iron Age, that is at some
date before 500 and after 900 B.C., and that the Bronze
Age script just overlaps into the Iron Age. That
Phoenician writing was also known in the Early Iron
Age is indicated by the vase No. 479 in the Cesnola
Collection which bears an early Phoenician inscription,
the name of an owner, incised on a red bucchero vase
after firing.

But the problem remains—to explain the extreme
paucity of examples of the script in the Dark Ages.

[1] Myres, p. 521, cf. p. 268, where it is suggested that they
belong to 'an earlier stage of the Syllabic script'.

Probably illiteracy was widespread and the knowledge of the script reverted to the hands of priests and bards. But that they kept it intact seems indicated by the re-emergence of a similar mode of writing when life became more settled and prosperous, even though no inscribed sacred object is known. In the same way during the Dark Ages of Great Britain the knowledge of writing Latin survived down to the ninth and tenth centuries, and the numerous but illiterate tombstones of Wales and western England testify to the fact that, when writing was needed, it was forthcoming.

The general linear and rectilinear character of the Classical Cypriot script taken together with the rough 16 per cent correspondences with the script of the Bronze Age suggest that the hypothesis, which we can hardly predicate on the evidence of correspondences alone, is a tolerable one. In an island where the coming of the Iron Age was followed by no overwhelming catastrophe it can hardly be a coincidence that the script used in the full Classical period was every bit as rectilinear in general character as its predecessor. The few curvilinear signs that appear may be due to a kind of contamination with Phoenician signs, since a knowledge of Phoenician was early in the field. The later signs Mo, Ro and Le adopt the fashionable curves of the day.

Myres remarks that the rectilinear forms of the Bronze Age script suggest that it 'was developed among carvers on wood'.[1] Attention has already been drawn to this above (p. 88). But what is so difficult to explain is the sudden popularity of the

[1] *Cesnola Catalogue*, p. 301.

script in the fifth century after a period of centuries when it might so easily have perished completely. Myres's further suggestion that the script re-emerged in a period when Cypriot nationalism was in the ascendant seems the most acceptable hypothesis, but it leaves unexplained the problem of how it survived in the interval between the Bronze Age and the fifth century, and why it 'did not actually expire altogether. Here a hint may be offered on the technical side. The adaptation of the script and perhaps the origin of it as a means mainly for inscribing on wood tablets or panels (as we know much Greek to have been inscribed in early times),[1] may allow us to infer that in the Bronze and Early Iron Ages it was widely so used— that is to say it was used on perishable material, for virtually no wooden object from these periods survives in Cyprus. Its use on vases and other objects was incidental, and, so used, it went out of fashion after the Bronze Age and survived mainly on wood. Thus we have lost the bulk of instances of its use. Alternatively, if we presume a growing illiteracy (for which in the Greek world in the Dark Ages there is overwhelming evidence), then we are driven to assume, if we reject the wood-usage hypothesis, that it reverted to the reserved usage of priests, princes and bards.[2]

[1] The laws of Solon were inscribed on ἄξονες of wood, Plutarch, *Solon*, 25.

[2] An analogy may be drawn from Ireland where Druids and their pupils studied an obsolete form of Goidelic Celtic and wrote it in Ogham Script. They preserved thus an almost forgotten language and an otherwise unknown vehicle for it. See R.A.S. Macalister, *The Secret Languages of Ireland*, Cambridge University Press, 1936.

These are all assumptions, mainly unsupported by reliable evidence ; but they derive support from the acknowledged and obvious conservatism and survival strength of Cypriot institutions, already fully documented in previous pages.

The only undisputed facts are that two types of script survived in Cyprus, one a Bronze Age script, of unknown but perhaps partly Minoan origin, the other of Classical times, strongly resembling the first in character. The latter was a syllabary, as we know from its translation by means of bi-lingual texts. We cannot do more than guess that the former also was a syllabary. If it was, then we are not far off being able to decipher some of the signs and groups of signs and give them sound values. But even when this is done we have no certain knowledge of the language which the prehistoric inscriptions hide. In Classical times the Cypriot script is used for at least one other language than Greek. Texts of considerable length survive (see above, p. 68) which are in a language or languages neither Phoenician nor Hellenic and hitherto unidentified. We have no certain reason as yet for thinking that the Bronze Age script represents the Greek language. But we have no certain reason for thinking that it does not, and the presence of large bodies of Achaean colonists in Cyprus in the Bronze Age strongly suggests that Greek was known in Cyprus in Mycenaean times. The one or more other languages which survive in the Classical script, may represent the pre-Achaean language of the pre-Mycenaean Cypriots, the aboriginal language itself. Whether the Bronze Age script was used for this language or for

pre-Dorian Greek we cannot tell. Possibly the fact
that the script is not in use before the advent of the
Mycenaean-Achaean colonists means that the script
was brought by or invented by them and so used for
their own language. Then, when it was later superseded by the Greek alphabet, which was a much more
practical vehicle of expression, the ancient and, by
then, characteristically Cypriot script, was relegated
for use in a more nationalistic stratum of society, and
so favoured by those who kept alive the aboriginal
language or wished to write Greek in a nationalistic
medium. It is naturally difficult to find a parallel for
this state of affairs, but one might say that there would
be a similar situation if Scottish Gaelic were to be
printed in Gothic type. The Gothic type was originally used for English, then discarded by the English
in favour of a more practical Latin type ; suppose
that then Scottish Nationalists, wishing to revive their
ancient Gaelic, chose an ancient mode of script, hal-
lowed by antiquity, but not really the original vehicle
of the national language which it was destined to
express.

Before closing this chapter it might be convenient
to mention a remarkable inscription which survives,
cut in the rock on the face of a cliff a few hundred
yards north of the village of Tokhni on the south coast
a few miles inland from Maroni, west of Larnaka. It
has the appearance of considerable antiquity and seems
quite authentic. It was seen and copied by Hogarth [1]
who remarks of it ' what it signifies, in what alphabet

[1] *Devia Cypria*, p. 109.

it is expressed, whether it is a date or magical formula or what else in the world, no one who has copied it has been able to determine '. I recopied it in the summer of 1933 and find that his copy is inaccurate in several details. But I can throw no more light on it than he could. The inscription is given below. The letters are, as when Hogarth saw it, painted in red ; but I suspect the local villagers, who take some pride in it, of keeping it freshly and regularly painted. All one can say is that the letters resemble Greek, Phoenician and Cypriot signs. The second sign could be a Greek digamma or the Cypriot syllable To ; the third seems Phoenician, the fourth and fifth could be Greek and the fifth either Greek or the Cypriot Sa. The last sign on the right looks Cypriot and the last but one Greek. More than that cannot be said. Perhaps it is an illiterate inscription inscribed by a local magician in ancient times, perhaps in classical days, to impress those who walked or worshipped in Tokhni ravine. I do not think it can be taken seriously or that it gives any contribution to knowledge. But an accurate copy of it is given here.

TOKHNI INSCRIPTION

I F ☐ϟΣΥ'Ϥ'ϯⴹ
I.

TABLE OF SIGNS OF THE BRONZE AGE SCRIPT ON OBJECTS FOUND IN CYPRUS

Note.—' Incised ' as used in this list in inscriptions on pottery means ' incised after the vase has been fired '.

SIGNS	SOUND VALUE IN CLASSICAL SCRIPT	PLACE WHERE FOUND	OBJECT ON WHICH SIGN IS INSCRIBED	REFERENCE	NUMBER OF EXAMPLES
1. ╪	pa	Karydhata	Pottery jug: incised on handle	Markides, *C.A.R.*, 1916, p. 16, No. 1	
		,,	Pottery jug: incised on handle	Op. cit., No. 2	
		Arpera	Incised on pithos fragment	Op. cit., No. 9	
		Enkomi	do.	Op. cit., No. 11, also Myres, *Man*, 1934 (Feb.); Evans, *P. of M.*, IV, ii, p. 759	10
		,,	Incised on handle of jar	*B.M. Cat.*, I, ii, p. 89, C. 430	
		Kurion	Painted on base of crater	*B.M. Cat.*, I, ii, p. 78, C. 391	
		Cyprus	False-necked Myc. vase	Cesnola Coll., Myres, No. 438	
		Enkomi	On clay ball	Persson, *a*	
		,,	do.	Persson, *b*	
		—	On shoulder of plain vessel	Cyprus Museum, No. 1462	

No.	Sign		Provenance	Description	Reference	No.
				handle	No. 3. No. 1494 in Cyprus Museum	2
			Klavdia, near Larnaka	False-necked jar (painted on base)	B.M. Cat., I, ii, p. 102, C. 514	
3.	卅		Katydhata	Plain jug : incised on handle	Markides, C.A.R., 1916, p. 17, No. 4	1
4.	Ⴧ		„	Plain jug : incised on shoulder	Markides, C.A.R., 1916, p. 16, No. 1	3
			Enkomi	Painted on base of vase	Gjerstad, S.C.E., No. 52, Schaeffer, No. IX	
			Cyprus	do.	In B.M., No. 583 ; Schaeffer, No. XXI	
5.	⊓		Arpera	Incised on fragment of pithos	Markides, C.A.R., 1916, p. 17, No. 9	1
6.	Ж		Enkomi	Incised on pithos fragment	Markides, C.A.R., 1916, p. 18, No. 11	1
7.	釆		„	do.	Op. cit, Myres, *Man.*, 1934	1
8.	全		„	Painted on base of crater	Cyprus Museum (unpublished). The sign is 10 cm. in height	1
9.	全		Katydhata	Jug of plain ware : incised on handle	Markides, C.A.R., 1916, p. 16, No. 2	1
10.	全	? si	Enkomi	Incised on pithos fragment	Op. cit, No. 11	2
			„	False-necked jar : incised on handle	B.M. Cat., I, ii, p. 103, C. 523	
11.	Ẍ		Arpera	Incised on pithos fragment	Markides, C.A.R., 1916, p. 17, No. 9	1

SIGNS	SOUND VALUE IN CLASSICAL SCRIPT	PLACE WHERE FOUND	OBJECT ON WHICH SIGN IS INSCRIBED	REFERENCE	NUMBER OF EXAMPLES
12. ⋋	la	Karydhata	Jug of plain ware : incised on handle	Markides, C.A.R., 1916, p. 17, No. 5	3
		,, Larnaka (Hala Sultan Tekke)	do.	Op. cit., No. 6	
			Painted jar : incised on handle	B.M. Cat., I, ii, p. 90, C. 434. See No. 48 in this table	
13. ⋇		Karydhata	Plain jug : incised on handle	Markides, C.A.R., 1916, p. 16, No. 2	1
14. ⼤		Cyprus	Plain ware : incised on handle	No. 1501 in Cyprus Museum (unpublished)	1
15. ⅄		,,	do.	No. 1505 in Cyprus Museum (unpublished)	3
		,,	Painted on base of vase	Schaeffer, No. XV (Cyprus Museum)	
		,,	do.	Schaeffer, No. XIX. B.M. Cat., I, ii, C. 555	
16. ⊓		Enkomi	Plain ware : impressed before firing	No. 1593 in Cyprus Museum (unpublished). Date of acquisition, 1927	2
		Klavdia, near Larnaka	Impressed before firing on red wheel-made flask	B.M. Cat., I, ii, p. 34, C. 191	
17. ⇐	? si	Enkomi	Clay balls	Persson, b and d. Evans, P. of M., IV, ii, 760	4
		? Larnaka	Bronze plaque	In private possession. Ashmol-	

No.	Sign		Locality	Description	Reference	Count
18.	𦘒		Cyprus	Plain ware: incised on handle	J.A.I., 1900, p. 215, Fig. 12 No. 1502 in Cyprus Museum (unpublished)	1
19.			"	do.	do.	1
20.			"	Plain jug: incised on handle	(on same vessel as preceding) No. 1492 in Cyprus Museum (unpublished)	1
21.			"	do.	(on same vessel as preceding)	1
22.			Maroni	Fragment of large painted crater: incised on handle	B.M. Cat., I, ii, p. 75, C. 379. Possibly this is a combination of two signs	1
23.		na	Arpera	On fragment of pithos	Markides, C.A.R., 1916, p. 17, No. 9	
			Larnaka	Gold ring	Evans, Scripta Minoa, p. 70, Fig. 38	4
			Cyprus	Red wheel-made vase	Cesnola Coll., Myres, p. 41, No. 377	
			"	Seal-cylinder	Ward, Seal-cylinders of Western Asia, No. 1164; Cesn. Coll., 4311	
24.			Enkomi	Clay ball	Persson, a	
			Arpera	Incised on pithos fragment	Markides, C.A.R., 1916, p. 17, No. 9 (Museum No. 1508)	3
			Cyprus	Seal-cylinder	Ward, No. 1164, loc. cit.; Cesn. Coll., 4311	

SIGNS	SOUND VALUE IN CLASSICAL SCRIPT	PLACE WHERE FOUND	OBJECT ON WHICH SIGN IS INSCRIBED	REFERENCE	NUMBER OF EXAMPLES
25. ⊓	? ra	Enkomi	Clay ball	Persson, b	1
26. +	lo	,,	do.	Persson, a	
		Cyprus	Incised on red wheel-made vessel	Cesnola Coll., Myres, p. 41, No. 378	
		Klavdia, near Larnaka	Painted on base of crater	B.M. Cat., I, ii, p. 84, C. 412	6
		? Larnaka	Bronze plaque	Replica in Ashmolean Museum. In private possession	
		Enkomi	Painted on base of vase	No. 1546 in Cyprus Museum; Schaeffer, No. V	
		,,	do.	Schaeffer, No. X (from Swedish excavations)	
27. ⊢	ta	,,	Clay ball	Persson, d (not identified by him)	
		Kurion	False-necked vase : incised on each of 2 handles	B.M. Cat., I, ii, p. 99, C. 501 (2 signs)	
		Enkomi	False-necked jar : incised on one handle	B.M. Cat., I, ii, p. 103, C. 523	6
		? Larnaka	Bronze plaque	Original in private possession. Replica in Ashmolean Museum	
		Enkomi	Painted on base of Mycenaean crater	Cyprus Museum (unpublished). This sign measures	

No.	Sign	Provenance	Object	Reference	No.
28.	⊔	Enkomi	Clay ball	Persson, a	1
29.	米 (e)	"	do.	Persson, b	2
		"	do.	Persson, d	1
30.	↙	Arpera	Plain vase: incised on handle	Markides, C.A.R., 1916, p. 18, No. 10	1
31.	¦¦	Katydhata	Plain jug: incised round mouth	Markides, C.A.R., 1916, p. 16, No. 1	
		Arpera	Plain vase: incised on handle	Markides, C.A.R., 1916, p. 18, No. 10	
		Cyprus	Incised on vase of red wheel-made ware	Cesnola Coll., Myres, p. 41, No. 381	3
32.	⋎	Enkomi	Clay ball	Persson, a	1
33.	米	"	do.	Persson, a (twice)	2
34.	米 or 米	"	do.	Persson, c and e (5th sign) = Evans, S.M., p. 71, No. 11, and P. of M., No. 7	
		Cyprus	Seal-cylinder	Ward, Seal-cylinders of Western Asia, No. 1164; Cesn. Coll., 4311	3
35.	ⵔ	Arpera	Pithos fragment	Markides, C.A.R., 1916, p. 17, No. 9	1
36.	人	Cyprus	False-necked painted vase: incised on handle	Cesnola Coll., Myres, p. 49, No. 438 and p. 525	
		Enkomi	Fragment of pithos	Markides, C.A.R., 1916, p. 18, No. 11, and Evans, P. of M., IV, 2, p. 759 (here shown as △), and Myres, Man, 1934 (Feb.)	2

SIGNS	SOUND VALUE IN CLASSICAL SCRIPT	PLACE WHERE FOUND	OBJECT ON WHICH SIGN IS INSCRIBED	REFERENCE	NUMBER OF EXAMPLES
37. ⟨sign⟩		Cyprus	Incised on vessel of red wheel-made ware	Cesnola Coll., Myres, p. 41, No. 376	1
38. ⟨sign⟩	? mo	,,	Incised on painted Mycenaean cup	Cesnola Coll., Myres, p. 47, No. 434	2
		Enkomi	Seal-cylinder	Dussaud, *Civilis. préhell.*, p. 429, No. 5 on list; *Exc. in Cyp.*, Pl. IV, 744	
39. ⟨sign⟩		Cyprus	False-necked vase : incised on handle	Cesnola Coll., Myres, p. 49, No. 438	1
40. ⟨sign⟩		,,	Incised on red wheel-made vessel	Cesnola Coll., Myres, p. 41, No. 379	1
41. ⟨sign⟩		Katydhata	Incised round mouth of white jug	Markides, *C.A.R.*, 1916, p. 16, No. 1. Possibly a numeral	1
42. ⟨sign⟩		Cyprus	Incised on handle of Mycenaean painted ? crater	In Cyprus Museum. Acquired in 1933 (unpublished)	1
43. ⟨sign⟩		Larnaka	Gold ring	Evans, *S.M.*, p. 70, and *P. of M.*, IV, ii, p. 759. It is uncertain if this ring is prehistoric	1
44. ⟨sign⟩	? le	,,	Seal-cylinder	Op. cit.	1
45. ⟨sign⟩	? vo	Cyprus	do.	Ward, *Seal-cylinders of Western Asia* No 1161; *Gems Coll*	2

46. Ͱ	Cyprus	do.	No. 5 in his list; *Exc. in Cyp.*, Pl. IV, 744	
	,,	do.	Louvre. Dussaud, *Civilis. préhell.*, p. 429, Fig. 319 Delaporte, *Cat. des Cyl. Orient* (Bibl. Nat.), No. 478	4
	,,	Painted on base of Mycenaean vase	Schaeffer, *Missions en Chypre*, No. VIII. In Cyprus Museum	1
	,,	Painted on base of Mycenaean vase	Schaeffer, op. cit., No. XIV. In Cyprus Museum	
47. 田	Enkomi	Seal-cylinder	Dussaud, *Civilis. préhell.*, p. 429, No. 5 in list. *Exc. in Cyp.*, Pl. IV, 744	1
48.	Larnaka (Hala Sultan Tekke)	Incised on handle of three-handled jar	See No. 12 in this table. *B.M. Cat.*, I, ii, No. C. 434	2
	Cyprus ?	Seal-cylinder	Dussaud, *Civilis. préhell.*, p. 431, Fig. 330	
49.	Larnaka (Hala Sultan Tekke)	Incised on handle of fragment of painted vessel	In British Museum (unpublished)	1
50.	,,	do.	do.	1
51.	,,	do.	do.	1
52.	Cyprus	Painted on base of large Mycenaean vase	Peabody Museum, Harvard University	1

SIGNS	SOUND VALUE IN CLASSICAL SCRIPT	PLACE WHERE FOUND	OBJECT ON WHICH SIGN IS INSCRIBED	REFERENCE	NUMBER OF EXAMPLES
53. H		Cyprus	Painted on base of vase	Schaeffer, No. VI; No. 1543 in Cyprus Museum	1
54.		Enkomi	do.	Schaeffer, No. VII	1
55.		,,	do.	Schaeffer, No. XI; S.C.E, No. 52	1
56.		Cyprus	do.	Schaeffer, No. XII	1
57.	le	,,	do.	Schaeffer, No. XIII	1
58.		Maroni	do.	Schaeffer, No. XVII; B.M. Cat., I., ii, C. 477	1
59.		? Cyprus	Seal-cylinder	Dussaud, Civilis. préhell., p. 436, Fig. 320	1
60.		,,	do.	Delaporte, Cat. des Cyl. Orient (Bibl. Nat.), No. 478	1
61.		,,	do.	do.	1

NUMERALS, &c.

			Division between groups of signs	
—	—	—		
|	Arpera	Incised series of 7 signs on pithos fragment	Markides, C.A.R., 1916, p. 17, No. 9. Used twice in this inscription	5
	Enkomi	Clay ball	Persson, *a*, used twice	
	„	do.	Persson, *b*, used once	
||'	Katydhata	Incised on handle of plain white vessel	Markides, C.A.R., 1916, p. 17, No. 6	1
≡	„	Incised on mouth of plain white jug	Markides, C.A.R., 1916, p. 16, No. 1	1
|||	„	Incised on handle of plain jug	Markides, C.A.R., 1916, p. 17, No. 7 (with preceding on same handle)	2
||||	„	Incised on handle of plain vessel	Markides, C.A.R., 1916, p. 17, No. 8	1

A PALESTINIAN GROUP

A small group of six signs inscribed on vases has been found during excavations at Tell Abu Hawam, in Palestine.[1] The vases inscribed are all Mycenaean, of various shapes, and are almost certainly imports from Cyprus. The quantity of contemporary Cypriot wares found in the same levels is sufficient support for this assumption. At the same time until it is certain that there were not factories for the manufacture of Mycenaean wares in Palestine, and a local use of the Cypriot script, perhaps with local variations, it would seem safer to give this Palestinian group separately from the Cypriot. All the signs in the preceding list come from objects found exclusively in Cyprus.

The appearance of Cypriot signs in the Palestinian group and the general similarity in type to the Cypriot makes it most probable that we have to deal with direct imports of Cypriot Mycenaean vases inscribed in Cyprus or in Palestine by people who habitually used the Cypriot script. The signs are in four cases inscribed in the place usual in Cyprus for such marks. In one case the sign is painted on the base in the manner of our Class I (1)*b*, which, as Professor Schaeffer has pointed out, indicates a class of pottery peculiar to Cyprus and marked in a manner which suggests a specific Cypriot workshop.

But until the possibility of a Cypriot colony in Palestine or Syria, where the same habit of painting

[1] I am indebted to Mr. W. A. Heurtley for calling my attention to this group. They are published in the *Quarterly of the Dept. of Antiquities in Palestine*, IV, p. 53.

and incising signs on vases existed, is ruled out, it would be wiser to class the Palestinian group separately. I have added to these eight ceramic examples of script signs, one where the sign is cut on stone. The seven signs are as follows :

1. ‡ Incised on a 3-handled jar and a false-necked vase. Two examples. The Cypriot sign No. 1.

2. ꟺ · Incised on the handle of a large painted 3-handled jar.

3. ⊦ Incised on the handle and base of a large 3-handled jar. Two examples. The Cypriot sign No. 27.

4. ⋈ Painted on the base of a bowl.

5. Y Incised on the handle of a jar.

6. + Incised near the base of a vase. Not certainly a sign, but if so, is the Cypriot No. 26.

7. ᴧ Cut on a stone weight.

It will be observed that out of these seven signs three are instances of the commonest signs in the Cypriot script of the Bronze Age. The rest conform closely to the general rectilinear character of the script. No. 2 is of the type of the Cypriot No. 12. No. 5 also resembles it. But they are distinct signs and, indeed, in this Palestinian group we may well find four new signs to add to our Cypriot total. But at the moment it is wiser to classify them separately.

CHAPTER IV

ALASIA

FROM 1600 B.C. to 1200 trade intercourse with Egypt is everywhere evident in Cyprus, becoming more intense as time proceeds. Datable scarabs [1] and other objects make it possible to follow the growth of Egyptian imports. In Egyptian documents there is mention of a place named Asî or ALASIA in various documents, particularly in eight of the letters of Tell-el-Amarna.[2] A king of Alasia is mentioned in the correspondence with Amenophis, whose date was from 1386 to 1368. The name Alasia was first suggested as that of Cyprus by Max Muller [3] who found its Cypriot counterpart surviving in the bilingual inscription, in Greek and Phoenician, from Tamassos,

[1] The greatest caution should be used when scarabs are the sole indications of date ; of *S.C.E.*, ii, Text, p. 818. At St. Irene scarabs of the Hyksos period and the XVIIIth Dynasty were found in the same stratification with scarabs of the XXVIth Dynasty. This stratum is clearly dated only by the scarabs of the XXVIth Dynasty. But had the later scarabs not been found, by the sheer accident of excavation the earlier date would, wrongly, have been fixed if the scarabs alone were the criterion. Obviously scarabs can only be used as corroborative evidence.

[2] J. A. Knudtzon, *Die El-Amarna Tafeln*, Nos. 33-40, and H. Winckler, *The Tell-el-Amarna Letters*, 25-32.

[3] *Zeitschrift fur Assyr.*, 1895, p. 257 ff.

where dedication is made to Ἀπόλλωνι τῶι Ἀλασιώται.
The name is thought to survive down to to-day in
the place-names Alassos and Ailasuka.[1] On the other
hand, Wainwright[2] identifies Alasia/Asî in North
Syria. On this point opinion has varied considerably,
but the recently added information from Hittite
sources seems to strengthen the Cypriot identification.
For the Hittite annals record commercial relations
with a region from which the Hittites imported
copper, and the name can be attached to it.[3] In the
late fifteenth century Alasia appears in the Hittite
political sphere for the first time. After the assassination of King Todhalias II (c. 1400) his brothers are
sent to Alasia in exile.[4] A century and a half later
King Hattosili sIII (c. 1290–1260), who seems to have
taken over the island from his predecessor Movatallis
(c.1307–1290), proscribes his political enemies in Alasia.[5]
Hattosilis concludes a treaty with Ramses II after the
battle of Kadesh in 1288 B.C. and it is probably the
same king who boasts in an inscription that ' the land
of Alasia is mine '.[6] Kadesh meant a certain retreat
on the part of Egyptian influence in the Levant and
Cyprus might well have fallen now into the Hittite
sphere.

[1] Oberhummer in P-W. (s.v. Kypros) for references.

[2] Klio, xiv, p. 1 ff., places Alasia/asi in North Syria.

[3] Winckler, Mitth. deutsch Orient. Gesell., 1907, p. 41, and
Sommer, Zeitschrift fur Assyr., 1921, p. 95.

[4] Forrer, Forschungen, ii, 1926, p. 11. S. Przeworski, ' Grecs et
Hittites : L'état actuel du problème ', Eos, xxx, 1927 (Leopoli),
p. 428.

[5] Götze, Mitth. Vorderas. Aegypt. Gesell., 1925, p. 25.

[6] Forrer, Mitth. deutsch Orient. Gesell., 1921, p. 32.

The foregoing evidence points to the fact that, at the time when Achaean immigration was filling up Cyprus with the Mycenaean mode of life, Cyprus was nominally under the tutelage of the Hittites of the opposite coast. As Achaean influence increased, this hold seems to have weakened and the Hittite king Arnuvandas III finds his island raided by the Achaean Atarssiyas accompanied by his vassal who is strangely named the ' man of Biggaya '. It is generally assumed that Biggaya is another name for Cyprus or part of the island, on grounds of general context, and also on particular grounds of etymology.[1] Atarssiyas, together with his companion, seems to have attempted to usurp the control of the island and used it as a base for raiding the Cilician coast as well, to the annoyance of the Hittite king. In the Hittite texts from the Boghaz Keui tablets, in which the name of Alasia occurs, the name is used with the prefix ' City of . . .' It was the Hittite custom to refer to other lands by the name of their capital cities or else to use the phrase ' The Land of the City of X '. Here it seems more briefly to have been used as ' City of . . .', meaning, in fact, the land itself. The same mode of appellation was in use also in Egypt, where a relief showing the assault on a Canaanitish city bears an

---

[1] Bowra, *Tradition and Design in the Iliad*, p. 166. Stephanus of Byzantium gives as one of the alternative names of Cyprus the name Σφήκεια which Forrer equates with Biggaya. In Forrer's map, in *Mitth. d. d. Orientgesell. zu Berlin*, 1924, No. 63, Biggaya is put as the north coast of Cyprus. Atarssiyas is called the ' Man from Ahhia '. Ahhia and Ahhiyava are hardly to be distinguished. But this definition of Atarssiyas suggests that Ahhiyava and Alasiots were by no means identical.

inscription describing the city as the ' City of Canaan '.[1]
Alasia can thus be legitimately considered as the Hittite
and Egyptian name in use for the island, if we reject
Wainwright's assumption that it was a region of Syria.[2]
It is accepted in 1930 as the name of Cyprus by
F. Bork and by Schachermeyer in 1935.[3] We can
now add the Syrian appellation of Cyprus from the
Ras Shamra texts. It here occurs as Alšy.[4]

The neighbouring island of Rhodes seems also to
have fallen into the sphere, both of the Achaean power
and of the Hittite. There is as yet no evidence to
suggest that it was an actual Hittite province, but
Professor Sayce pointed out that one proper name
in the Boghaz Keui texts was the unusual name Ata-
burussiyas, which he suggests is connected with the
very unhellenic name of a mountain, Mount Atabyris,
in Rhodes.[5]

It would not be possible to examine the problems

[1] Ebert, *Reallexicon*, iii, p. 90.
[2] A further argument against Wainwright's location of Alasia
in Syria, suggested by O. Davies in *B.S.A.*, xxx, p. 81, is that
another name for Cyprus should be forthcoming in the Egyptian
texts, and there is none. The argument in support of Wainwright
offered by Davies, that Alasia exported lead and ivory, seems base-
less. Mycenaean Cyprus was rich in ivory and Davies produces
sufficient evidence for the presence of lead in the island (e.g.
Dioscorides, v, 75). He forgets that Cyprus could have acted as
middleman in both cases.
[3] F. Bork, *Die Sprache von Alasia.* Schachermeyer, *Hethiter
u. Achäer*, p. 69, who notes that E. Meyer, Bilabel, Sommer
Hrozny and Forrer also accept it.
[4] See *Syria*, x, 1929, Pl. 62, 21, 29.
[5] *Transactions of the Classical Association in Oxford*, 1928, No. VI,
p. 1.

that concern Rhodes in this book. But it is clear
that Rhodes and Cyprus stand in a very close relation
in Mycenaean times. Rhodes had a Mycenaean
period as intense and active as that of Cyprus. The
island was almost certainly a secondary centre of
Mycenaean production and there is no reason to
think that Mycenaean wares in Rhodes were imports
from the Greek mainland ; indeed, there are peculiar
features of Mycenaean vases in Rhodes which suggest
local manufacture. Nor is there much resemblance
between the general Mycenaean style of Rhodes
and that of Cyprus. The chariot-scene vases are
hardly found there, but the ' non-composed' style of
Cyprus appears in neighbouring islands.[1] Rhodes
and the Dodecanese may perhaps be considered to
have a particular taste for bull-headed cups. One
from Carpathos [2] and one from Rhodes [3] show a type
of vessel not paralleled in the mainland at many
places and here treated to a luxuriant adornment of
decoration, differing in each case.[4] But none are
recorded from Mycenae.

There is also a type of vessel common at Rhodes

[1] As in *B.M. Cat.*, I, i, No. A. 1022 from Calymnos, almost
sub-Mycenaean, while A. 1015 from Calymnos is in similar vein.
It is interesting that an almost identical vase (probably an import)
was found at Pitane in Aeolis (see *B.M.C.*, loc. cit., p. 194).

[2] *B.M. Cat.*, I, i, A. 971.

[3] Jacopi, *Museo Arch. di Rodi.*, 1932, p. 93, Fig. 51.

[4] Possibly the Levantine Mycenaean wares of Rhodes and
Cyprus favoured animal forms just as they favoured animal
designs. The pig from Troy (H. Schmidt, Schliemann-Samm-
lung, No. 3563) may be for this reason an import from the Levant
and not from the mainland.

which has been isolated as a characteristic Rhodian-
Mycenaean fabric peculiar to the island.[1] It consists
of large craters and amphorae decorated with repre-
sentations of wild goats. These are not found either
in Cyprus or at Ras Shamra.[2] One is recorded as a
stray importation from Rhodes back to the Greek
mainland.[3]

But the fundamental difference between the
Mycenaean culture of Rhodes and that of Cyprus is
that in Rhodes the Achaean intruders seem to have
arrived as conquerors, rather than as colonists. For
after their arrival there seems to have been no sub-
stantial survival of anything which we might call
'native Rhodian' elements, whereas in Cyprus, as
has been abundantly made clear, the native element
persists vigorously side by side with the Mycenaean,
and the colonists adopted Cypriot burial customs and
grave-types. Nothing of the kind seems to have
occurred in Rhodes.[4] That Rhodes was fully
occupied or perhaps conquered by Achaeans before
the arrival of the Dorians who so thoroughly dorianized the island, is further indicated by the title of, Ἀχαία
πόλις which was given, presumably at the time of the
Dorian occupation, to Ialysos.[5]

The presence of Hittites in Cyprus, or indications
of trade and other relations, are as scanty as they are

[1] Schachermeyer, op. cit., pp. 102 and 110.
[2] Idem, p. 110.
[3] At Asine (in the Nauplia Museum). Schachermeyer, op. cit.,
p. 102, n. 1.
[4] For a general summary of the position see Schachermeyer,
op. cit., p. 98 ff.
[5] Schachermeyer, op. cit., p. 99, n. 2.

in every region where Hittite connexions are known and recorded. The continuous connexions of Hittites with Ahhiyava-Achaeans, so fully documented by the recently deciphered Boghaz-Keui tablets, finds only a minute and hesitating archaeological confirmation. And yet the tablets are not to be doubted, nor is the equation Achaean-Ahhiyava in dispute by reputable scholars. Mainland Greece, although it was in extensive touch with Hittites through its various expeditionary forces and colonizing bodies, seems to have absorbed almost nothing from the Hittites. The known Hittite objects from Mainland Greece are in no case satisfactory documents and in number are not even a handful. So, too, in Cyprus the Hittite connexions have left a sparse archaeological commentary.

But it is more than can be provided elsewhere. Evans, long since,[1] called attention to the peculiar characteristics of the scenes depicted on the well-known ivory draught-box from Enkomi. Although the form of the box itself is Egyptian, the design of an archer mounted in a galloping chariot suggests Hittite and Syrian parallels. On the Rekhmere paintings the same type of chariot is seen driven by Syrians and in the frescoes of Ramses II representing the battle of Kadesh, Hittite warriors are driving similar chariots. In short, the ivory has strong Hittite affinities. A warrior attacking a griffin on the same box carried arms which are similar to those on the late Hittite reliefs.

But only one Hittite object of first-rate importance

[1] *J.A.I.*, 1900, p. 210.

PLATE VII

LOOKING NORTHWARDS TOWARDS ANATOLIA, OVER THE SITE OF LAPETHOS AND THE COASTAL
PLAIN, BELOW THE NORTHERN MOUNTAIN RIDGE

has been found in Cyprus—a gold Hittite seal bearing an inscription in Hittite.[1] It comes from Tamassos and is in the Ashmolean Museum. But Cypriot connexions with the Anatolian coast across the Caramanian strait have recently been more fully illustrated. Gjerstad,[2] after examining many coastal sites in Cilicia has come to the following conclusions :

(a) that Late Mycenaean (which he calls Helladic) wares are scattered fairly evenly along the coast ;

(b) that there is an imitation of this which he calls Hellado-Cilician. It is not an import from Greece and the question arises whether it is made in Cilicia or in some neighbouring land. He decides that it was made in Cilicia and then asks the question, ' Was it made in Cilicia by Mycenaeans or by Cilicians in imitation of genuine Mycenaean ware ? ' He decides in favour of its manufacture by immigrant Mycenaeans.

This final question is vitiated by his assumption that Mycenaean wares could only have been made by Mycenaeans coming from Greece. For this there is evidence enough, such as the story of Bellerophon in the Aleian plain, and the legend that Mopsos and Amphilochos settled in these regions. They are said to have founded the city of Mallus, where also was a famous oracle of Amphilochos. Famous characters of the Mycenaean Age seem to have had much to do in Cilicia, and these legends, he thinks, reflect the activities of mainland Mycenaeans. But since in

[1] Hogarth, *Hittite Seals*, No. 191.
[2] *Revue Archéologique*, 1934, p. 155, ' Cilician studies ' ; Schachermeyer, op. cit., p. 116 ff.

9

regard to Cyprus, he has rejected any theory of an Achaean colonization (see above, p. 46), he is forced to bring the Mycenaean elements in Cilicia direct from Greece. Now the Cilicians are said by Herodotus [1] to have been called Ὑπαχαιοί. Whether this can be interpreted, as it has been,[2] as 'Achaeans of the Lowlands' is open to grave dispute. In any case it seems to amount to a term indicating a smaller branch or settlement of the Achaean race. This at least is hardly in dispute. Gjerstad leaves undecided the important problem of whether these Cilician Achaeans had moved over from Cyprus.[3] And there is evidence to suggest that this was the case, and that it was a late movement from Cyprus north to Anatolia. Hesiod,[4] surely the earliest possible evidence, recording an event not far off his own age, states that Amphilochos died at Soloi in Cyprus. But it is almost impossible to conclude that two quite separate movements of Achaeans came from Greece (to Cyprus on the one hand and to Cilicia on the other) in view of the

[1] VII, 91.

[2] Gjerstad, loc. cit., quoting Sommer. Burn, in *Minoans, Philistines and Greeks*, p. 121, suggests as comparison with Ὑποθῆβαι in the Iliad (ii. 505), which means 'Lower Thebes' or 'Thebes below the citadel'.

[3] Schachermeyer, op. cit., p. 124, dates the arrival of Achaeans in Cilicia to the first half of the fourteenth century. He rejects Gjerstad's view that Cypriot Mycenaean wares were imports from Cilicia. This latest variation of Gjerstad's general view of importation, so developed, (see *Rev. Arch.*, 1934, p. 195 ff.) is virtually a *reductio ad absurdum* of the whole theory.

[4] Quoted by Strabo, xiv, 5.17. Ἡσίοδος δ' ἐν Σόλοις ὑπὸ Ἀπόλλωνος ἀναιρεθῆναι τὸν Ἀμφίλοχόν φησιν.

fact that between 1240 and 1225 Atarssyas is apparently based on Cyprus raiding Cilicia. Cyprus was certainly the goal of a great colonizing movement from the mainland by 1350 at the latest, and Atarssyas came to an island partly but not necessarily wholly Achaeanized. He, like other Achaeans, used it for raiding the coast opposite, which, after all, was visible to the naked eye and an alluring goal for adventurers.

Gjerstad places this settlement of Cilicia at the very end of the Bronze Age and at the beginning of the Iron Age [1] because most of the traditions of Achaean enterprise are connected with the fall of Troy and the period immediately following. But the Bellerophon legend must belong to a very early age, hardly later than 1350, for it presupposes a full knowledge of Minoan script ; in any case it seems to reflect conditions long preceding the Trojan war. Bellerophon himself belongs to a later time than the setting of the story or its form. The story is an ancient folk-tale. This legend is concerned with the one area—the Aleian plain—where Gjerstad found the Hellado–Cilician ware to be most common. In effect, the Aleian plain was the region most populated by Achaeans, and because of its fertility the region longest sought after and known. There was thus a longer history to Achaean or Mycenaean development of Cilicia than Gjerstad would admit.

That it was Mycenaean Achaeans from Cyprus who largely opened up this coast to development is indicated by the general historical situation as well as the Hittite records. The discovery of a fragment

[1] Op. cit., p. 200.

of a chariot vase of characteristic Cypriot fabric on the same coast [1] is significant.

This main theory that Cypriot Mycenaeans rather than mainland Mycenaeans were largely responsible for this northern encroachment on Hittite coasts is strengthened by the fact that Cypriot activities are also recorded on the North Syrian coast. The Aleian plain is just across the gulf of Alexandretta from Mount Casios, near which is Ras Shamra, the recently excavated Syrian site which has revealed so many Aegean and Cypriot connexions. The Byzantine chronographer Malalas [2] records that this Casios-Shamra region was colonized by a certain King Casos from Cyprus and that the town so built was called Amyke. This is probably the Greek name of Shamra, though the name it bore in the Bronze Age, from the evidence of the Shamra tablets is Ugarit. The Cypriot king Casos, who inaugurated this eastern move, was himself of Argive origin, having come from the Argolid to Cyprus. He brought with him on his enterprise Cretans as well. As Dussaud says,[3] ' the myths as well as the archaeological discoveries associate the settlement at Shamra with the Achaean Empire '. Among the discoveries were many imported Cypriot fabrics,[4] faience head-vases exactly similar to vases from Enkomi and Mycenaean vases of Cypriot type [5] ;

---

[1] Burton-Brown in *Liverpool Annals*, xx, p. 43 ff.

[2] VIII, p. 201.   [3] *Syria*, x, p. 303.

[4] *Syria*, xiv, 105, Pl. xi, 1 and xii, 3. Cf. Schachermeyer, op. cit., p. 108.

[5] Flat plates, cf. *Syria*, x, p. 18, fig. 1. Craters, cf. *Syria*, xii, Pl. iii, 2.

the general view held at present is that Shamra-Ugarit
was a city which was the principal medium of Cypriot-
Asiatic trade in the later Bronze Age. No doubt its
antiquity as a port cognizant of the Aegean peoples
went back much earlier, and there is reason to think
that it originally had Minoan connexions.[1] But the
Cypriot contacts are the most numerous and the legend
of King Casos points to a very definite Cypriot
exploitation which need not have been exclusively
Cypriot. Its position directly facing Mycenaean
Salamis in Cyprus suggests that the two ports were in
direct relation. Mount Casios is visible from the east
coast of Cyprus and would serve as a landmark for
those sailing to Syria. In the legend King Casos
married Kitia, the daughter of King Salaminos.
Virolleaud,[2] in discussing the remarkable cuneiform
alphabet found on tablets from Shamra, sees in
them a connexion with the later Cypriot syllabary.
But at present this is hardly more than a conjecture.

Cyprus thus seems to have played a very important
part in the Mycenaean expansion eastwards, the general
Achaean trend along the ancient trade route of the
Levant towards the rich trade centres of the Orient.
That the islanders made of their island a specific *entrepôt*
for communication between Syria and the west is
certain. That Cilicia came under Mycenaean influ-

[1] As illustrated by a fragment of Middle Minoan Kamares
ware found there in 1936.

[2] *Syria*, x, p. 309. The alphabet of Ras Shamra can hardly,
as he suggests, be the prototype of the Cypriot syllabary. The
Minoan-Mycenaean origin of the syllabary is demonstrable.

ence, which is not doubted, without their mediation, is almost inconceivable. Cyprus was, in fact, a centre from which radiated northwards and eastwards the culture and energy and enterprise of the Achaean colonists.

Casual mention only has so far been made of the importance of Cyprus as a source of copper in the Bronze Age. It has been assumed without argument that this was, in fact, the case. But a recent attempt to show that 'Cypriot copper mines were hardly worked in the prehistoric period'[1] and that the fame of Cyprus as a copper-island originated only in the Classical Age, demands some investigation.

The main arguments proposed are that the only specific positive evidence so far brought forward is insufficient or unsound. Thus the author of this thesis thinks that the literary evidence is valueless. But the literary evidence is, on the contrary, most specific. Some literary statements have, it is true, been forced to imply more than they permit, such as the bare statement in Homer that Cinyras of Cyprus gave to Agamemnon a fine corselet.[2] Whoever was foolish enough to use this event to prove that Cyprus was famed for its metal-work and consequently a great source of metallurgy in the Bronze Age, would have been better employed spinning fairy-tales. But the lines in the Odyssey [3] that describe the ship which sailed to 'alien-speaking folk to Temese with a cargo

[1] O. Davies in *B.S.A.*, xxx, p. 74 ff., 'The copper mines of Cyprus.'
[2] *Iliad*, XI, 20.   [3] *Odyssey*, I, 184.

of shining iron to fetch copper (or bronze) ' in its place, are to be taken much more seriously as indication of active copper-mining in Cyprus in the Late Mycenaean Age—on the assumption that Temese is to be identified with Tamassos. Controversy has raged over the question and in the end the main issue is a place-name identification based on similarity—always a hazardous enterprise. But in this case we must somehow find a place in the Mediterranean where iron would be welcome and copper common. The Temese-Tamassos equation is unusually tempting.[1] The alternative of Temesa = Tempsa in Bruttium, first proposed by Strabo,[2] is supported by O. Davies. The grounds for his support are that Homer's Temese is on the sea coast, while Tamassos is inland ; that the term ' folk of alien tongue ' could hardly apply to Cypriots after the Mycenaean immigration, and that iron is not known to have been worked west of Ithaka as early as this, while it is known in Greece and Asia Minor. He thus decides that the ship was sailing westwards from the east and not in the reverse direction.

These arguments may be met seriatim :

Tamassos is not on the coast. But no one expects such meticulous geography from Homer, nor indeed from any one. A shipowner might well ' send a ship to Carrara for marble ' without being expected

---

[1] The later Assyrian name for Tamassos in the eighth century was Tamisu (see Oberhummer in *P.W.* (*s.v.* Kypros), p. 102). This strengthens the equation, if value can be attached to the similarity Temese-Tamisu.

[2] VI, 1.5.

to haul his ship overland from the port to the quarries. The suggestion that Cypriots must all have talked Greek after the Mycenaean immigration, apart from making wide assumptions about the language of the Mycenaeans (which however I do not reject), ignores the fact that the Cypriot aboriginals were not exterminated by this immigration. So persistent were they that their language apparently survived late into the Classical Age. At least ἀλλόθροοι ἄνθρωποι lived their life in quite late times in the island and recorded their language on various inscriptions in the Classical Cypriot syllabary. The Homeric phrase is thus particularly appropriate to Cyprus.

Later, as Davies shows, Pliny[1] records that Cinyras was responsible for the origin of copper-mining; Strabo[2] that the Telchines discovered copper and iron working and migrated from Crete, after a stay at Rhodes, to Cyprus. Other authors give other tales of origins of metallurgy, but none are so authoritative as Pliny and Strabo, who, in generalizations like these, usually preserve the general beliefs of antiquity. Diodorus[3] remarks on the memory of Telchines being preserved at Rhodes in the cult of Apollo, Telchinios at Lindos and Hera Telchinia at Camiros. It seems more than a coincidence that a movement of people or individuals from Crete to Rhodes and then to Cyprus concerned with metallurgy should be referred to a remote past by the classical Greeks. It bears an unusual resemblance to the colonization movement which reached Rhodes and Cyprus in the Bronze Age. The passage from Strabo and that from

[1] N.H., vii, 56, 195.   [2] XIV, 2.7.   [3] V, 55.

Diodorus (which Davies ignores) cannot lightly be dismissed.

The argument that iron is not known west of Ithaka at this early time assumes that the cargo in question must necessarily have come from west of Ithaka. But it could equally have come from north of Ithaka from some Illyrian port in the Adriatic in touch with the iron workings of the Danube valley which were beginning about this time (c. 1100 ?). And this argument is, after all, based only on negative evidence.

Finally, the famous ingot from Enkomi [1] bearing a sign from the Cypriot script of the Bronze Age cannot be so lightly dismissed as Mr. Davies would suppose. He states, against the assumption that this ingot points to local manufacture, that the script-sign upon it is a sign not confined to Cyprus alone, and develops his general argument that the ingot was probably imported from Crete. But, apart from the weakness of the general theory, the sign is, in fact, a typical Cypriot sign (see above, Table of Signs, p. 101, No. 17) and occurs on the Larnaka bronze plaque and on one of the clay balls from Enkomi. In the form in which it here appears it is not identical with any sign in the Minoan script, though it is fairly close to Evans's sign No. B. 17 [2] of the Linear B script. And it does not occur at all on the mainland script.

[1] Murray, *Excavations in Cyprus*, p. 15. Davies refers to a second ingot of this type from Enkomi, 'from another hoard found recently and said to be Mycenaean'; this loose method of reference is intolerable in a scientific paper. I am unable to identify the ingot to which he refers.

[2] *P. of M.*, IV, ii, Fig. 666.

Furthermore, as evidence that the large Scouriotissa mines were worked in the Bronze Age, we have the large Mycenaean settlement of Katydhata,[1] of which Davies makes no mention at all, while Tamassos was famous in antiquity[2] for its copper mines and their particular by-product the ἰὸς τοῦ χαλκοῦ. Finally, he does not take into account the eight Amarna letters from a King of Alasia to the King of Egypt, in six of which the export of copper to Egypt is mentioned. The numerous grounds for the identification of Alasia with Cyprus bring these letters into the argument. Mr. Davies' rejection of the equation Alasia/Cyprus is as much necessitated by his theory as is its acceptance, as he claims, required by those who presuppose Cypriot copper to have been worked in the Bronze Age. As we have seen, there are stronger archaeological grounds for the equation.

The general view that one of the objectives of the Mycenaeans was a supply of copper—and conceivably also the iron of the Hittite lands—is adopted here. But that is quite a different matter from the view that the Cypriots were actually the first to discover the metallurgy of copper. That is tenable, and the ancients so some extent believed it, as we have seen. But it is on the whole more likely that it was first worked in Egypt. Hall[3] remarked that ' the comparative absence of Neolithic remains in Cyprus ' and our inability to trace back Cypriot culture to a date sufficiently early for Cyprus to have communicated her knowledge of metallurgy to Egypt, strengthens

[1] *Cyprus Annual Report*, 1916.   [2] Strabo, xiv, 6.5.
[3] *Civilization of Greece in the Bronze Age*, p. 33.

the case for the priority of Egypt. But now the discovery of an extensive Neolithic culture in Cyprus destroys this argument, in the way in which so many negative arguments are likely to perish. But the Neolithic culture of Cyprus has affinities with the north or west, and certainly not with Egypt, so that it rather looks as if Cyprus was wholly out of touch with Egypt during this Neolithic Age. This is a more powerful argument than the argument from negation. Gjerstad's view on this matter is reasonable. He thinks [1] that the working of copper was not a Cypriot invention at all, but came to Cyprus with the movement of peoples from Anatolia that heralded the Bronze Age of Cyprus with its distinctive red wares. The intruders arrived as copper-workers. Finally, if proof were needed that copper or bronze was worked in Cyprus, the large assortment of smelting instruments and instruments for beating metal found at Enkomi [2] should be sufficient.

Even if the certainty that Alasia is Cyprus is doubted, we cannot afford to ignore the statement in one of the Boghaz Keui texts [3] that 'from the city of Alasia, from Mount Taggata, copper has been brought'. With a rich copper-bearing island so close to the Hittite centres it seems unnecessary to

[1] *Civilization of Greece in the Bronze Age*, p. 33, n. 2.

[2] Murray, *Excavations in Cyprus*, p. 15.

[3] Schachermeyer, *Klio*, 1921, 238. Wainwright, *Antiquity*, 1936, p. 14, gives an alternative translation of the passage as 'copper and bronze from the city of Alasiya and Mount Taggata' which occurs in a list of materials and their places of origin, in which gold, silver and iron are mentioned. For an earlier translation see Sayce in *Man*, 1921, No. 97.

search the Syrian and Anatolian coast for insignificant copper mines. The text itself, without assuming our conclusion as proved, leads us to search for the richest local copper deposits ; this leads to an identification of Alasia with Cyprus, and of Cyprus as a centre of the copper industry.

I may, perhaps, close the chapter with an account of an enigmatic work of art that is said to come from the site of Kurion. It is in the British Museum. It is a bronze stand of the type already seen in two Mycenaean examples (see above, p. 55), presumably part of a more elaborate tripod. The four panels decorated with figure scenes *á jour*, are in a style which it is hard to classify. The formal decoration of the stand is apparently of pure Mycenaean style, but the figures in the panels are heavy and Oriental in appearance; I suspect Babylonian and Egyptian influence. One of the panels shows what is almost certainly a man carrying or holding two ivory tusks. A second panel shown here (Plate VIII) shows a scene less difficult to interpret. A man is carrying on his shoulders an object which closely resembles in shape the ordinary Bronze Age copper ingot of the Levant and Aegean. But he is holding its lower extremities by handles which are not part of the ingot. But carrying handles are known on the ingots shown on the coins of the Damastini [1] and it is conceivable that handles were attached to the corners of ingots to steady them when carried. The surface of the object here conjectured as an ingot is covered with a dotted design.

[1] Head, *Historia Numorum*, p. 318. *B.M. Cat. Coins*, Thessaly &c., XVI, 5.

PLATE VIII

BRONZE STAND SAID TO COME FROM KURION
PANEL SHOWING VOTARY CARRYING A (?) COPPER INGOT

Certainty of identification of the object is impossible, but if ivory is shown on one panel, there is
some likelihood that some other commodity exported
or re-exported from Cyprus may be shown on
another. If it is an ingot then we have further
presumptive evidence for the working of copper in
the island.[1]

[1] See R. D. Barnett in *Iraq*, 1935, p. 209. Mr. Barnett inter-
prets those two panels as a man bearing ' a cup and two napkins
of enormous length' and a man who ' brings a skin of wine '.
The remaining two panels are unambiguous and show a man
bringing an offering of fish and a man seated playing a harp. In
each panel a sacred tree rendered in a Mycenaean convention is the
object of attention by the devotee. Mr. Barnett's interpretations
of the two scenes referred to above are not convincing. The
date of the box is problematical, it has every appearance of being
Late Mycenaean rather than Phoenician.

CHAPTER V

CYPRUS IN THE DARK AGES

THE early existence in the Bronze Age of the kingdoms or principalities of Cyprus, I have already assumed to have been likely on the evidence of the Mycenaean origin of a majority of the sites of the Classical cities. This fact, coupled with the known Mycenaean social organization into small feudal kingships, suggests that it is the titles of these kingdoms which appear in the famous temple-inscription of Medinet Habu,[1] belonging to the first quarter of the twelfth century B.C. There is naturally doubt, as there always must be in the identification of place-names solely by resemblance of sound and form, that we have to do with a group of Cypriot cities, among those listed by Ramses III as tributary. But, the collocation of the names *Salomaski, Katian, Aimar, Sali, Ital, (M)aquas, Kerena* or *Kelena* and *Kir . . .* , give us the easy equation of Salamis, Kition, Marion, Soloi, Idalion, Akamas, Kerynia and Kurion. These cities in the Egyptian inscription are said to be cities of the Ha Nebu, a title specially assigned, at least in later times, to Greeks, though also used to designate Carians.[2] But since Anatolians of the south coast were, as we have seen, largely mixed with intrusive Achaeans and

[1] Evans, *Scripta Minoa*, p. 75.   [2] Evans, loc. cit.

Achaeo-Cypriots (see above, p. 119) this causes no difficulty. The inscription seems to point to the continuity of the kingdoms during the Late Bronze Age. But there are some noteworthy points in this list. The dubious (M)aquas-Akamas does not appear before or after as a kingdom ; nor does Kerynia, while Kition is, by the inscription, given an existence at a date rather earlier than we should have expected for a Phoenician city. But the next reference in time to Cyprus is in the famous Egyptian story of Wen Amon preserved in the Golenischeff papyrus of about 1100 B.C. at a time when the Levant was filled with piracy and the great age of raids and expeditions was beginning. Wen Amon sailed from Byblos and, escaping the Zakkarai pirates who lay in wait for him, ran into a southerly gale which finally wrecked his ship on Alasia. Here he was taken before a ruling queen, Hatiba. The fact that Wen Amon had to employ a local interpreter for his Egyptian shows that he was in a land where Egyptian was known sufficiently for an interpreter to be found easily, as would have been the case in Cyprus ; if Alasia is the Syrian coast such quick interpretation would have been improbable, for Cyprus had long had Egyptian connexions, while Egyptian contacts north of Palestine were only sporadic. A southerly gale could, of course, have driven Wen Amon's ship on to the Syrian coast, but it looks as if he had been wrecked on the south coast of Cyprus. The Queen Hatiba, whose name has been identified as Phoenician,[1] might possibly have been queen of Kition.

[1] Max Müller quoted in Evans, op. cit., p. 75, n. 7.

All evidence of this type is, however, problematical
and uncertain, and we must turn to the more solid
ground of archaeological facts. It is, as Myres points
out,[1] no coincidence that Tyre dates its history from
the year 1198, a date significantly near the age of
confusion of which the stories of Wen Amon and
records of disturbances in Philistia, which Ramses
prevented from spreading southwards, are typical.

The earliest archaeological record for Phoenician
activity in Cyprus is a vase[2] of Red Bucchero ware
which bears the name of its owner, incised after firing,
in Phoenician. This ware (Myres's Fabric XIV),
difficult to date, is certainly anterior to the sixth
century, and common in the first half of the Early
Iron Age. It may therefore fall into the period
1000–800. The next datable vase bearing an inscription is not met with until the sixth century.[3]

This is scant and almost useless evidence, for such
objects may have arrived as imports, but they should
be considered in relation to the wide Orientalizing
influence seen in the later Mycenaean minor works
of art, especially the ivories, which contain qualities
of style not truly Mycenaean.[4]

The most continuous Phoenician contact, however,
is to be found in the richly chased bowls of ‘ Mixed
Oriental ’ style which, because of the inability of their
artists ever to depict one pure style, forces us to
assign them to the one people who in antiquity

---

[1] *Cesnola Collection*, p. xxxi.   [2] Cesnola Collection, No. 479.
[3] Ibid., No. 775 a bowl of Fabric XVI with an inscription in
paint made before firing.
[4] Evans, op. cit., p. 69.

learned the trick of 'pastiche' without contributing any element of their own native style. There is, however, one example from Cyprus, now in Berlin,[1] of a silver bowl of pure Egyptian manufacture, dated to the XIXth/XXth Dynasty—about 1200 B.C. It was found by Cesnola. A group of three more[2] reflects the Egyptian style of the period between the XIXth and XXVIth Dynasties. The probability that they are, in date, near to the Berlin bowl is remote, for bowls of this type found elsewhere are rarely dated before 700. Moreover, one of these bowls, No. 4552, in the Cesnola Collection bears an inscription in the Classical script, which is read—e.pi.o.ro. ti.e.a.pi.a.la.e., which is transliterated into Greek thus Ἐπιώρω Διεῦ ἁ φιάλα ἠ(μί). Since all inscriptions on metal can be made by an owner after purchase there is no indication here of local manufacture. The use of the fully developed Classical script makes it improbable that this bowl antedated 600 B.C., although Myres classes it with the earliest group. If it actually antedates 600 then it preserves the earliest known instance of a fully fledged version of the Classical script, and it would be remarkable that out of the many early metal objects none except this bore inscriptions in the script.

As Myres points out, these bowls may derive from several local schools which may have grown up either in Cyprus or in Phoenicia and Syria. Their prototype may be seen in a gold bowl from Ras Shamra

[1] Myres, *Cesnola Catalogue*, p. 457.
[2] Ibid., Nos. 4551-3. No. 4551 is of gold, No. 4552 of silver and No. 4553 of both metals.

10

dated to the fourteenth century B.C.[1] The design on this bowl is zoned, like the designs on the later bowls, but the style is more Cypro-Hittite than Phoenician. What is certain is that the bowls travelled widely and that their presence denotes trade and not settlement. They are found in the early Orientalizing period at Delphi, Athens and Olympia, and in Italy at Caere and Praeneste : they influenced the metal-work of Bologna and southern Austria in the Early Iron Age and were of great popularity throughout the Mediterranean. One was also found at Salerno. Cyprus, however, has the majority. In addition to the Egyptian Berlin example and the three in New York of the earliest type, there are six more, fragmentary or complete, in New York, of silver (Nos. 4554–9) and two (Nos. 4560–1) of bronze. All are decorated with a chased design in great detail of Egyptianizing and Assyrianizing subjects. One, No. 4556, surviving in fragments, is remarkable in that it is an almost exact replica of a well-preserved example from Praeneste.[2] Both are undoubtedly from the same studio. Such exact duplication is non-existent in Greek art, but apparently a Phoenician tendency. That a deeply commercial people should also develop the principles of mass-production is normal. The extraordinary character

[1] *Syria*, 1934. Pl. xv.

[2] Myres, op. cit., p. 464, and Marquand, *A.J.A.*, iii, p. 322. The differences are of composition rather than of style, and are only in minor details. The Cypriot example seems to have a different design on the second zone, but it is too fragmentary to establish the difference exactly. The main story is clearly the same in the outer zone and differences of detail are in trifling things only, such as landscape features.

of the designs on this Cypriot bowl and the astonishing legend recorded in the design [1] make it and its counterpart in Praeneste of peculiar interest. The story told is a kind of epic, Homeric in quality, of the adventures of a king who goes into the wilderness to hunt, and encounters a Wild Man of the Mountains. The complete story is preserved on the Praeneste example.

Probably most of these bowls date to before 600, but there is no reason to suppose that any of them falls into that dim period of uncertainty that followed the fall of Mycenaean power in Greece and Crete. For such precious and expensive works of art demand a settled society and wealthy purchasers. In the period between 1100 and 800 there were neither. That alone is a strong argument against the earlier dating. Thus we have the one solitary Egyptian gold bowl which belongs to the end of a period of civilization and the others which belong to the beginning of a new age.

What exactly was the condition of Cyprus after the catastrophe which befell Old Greece and the whole Aegean we cannot for certain tell. The almost complete failure of the script in this dark age points to the increase of illiteracy and poverty. But there is no catastrophe and no break in continuity in Cyprus, merely a loss of contact with the outside world and a determination to remain insular and independent. The Greek tradition assigned to Cyprus

[1] The two bowls have recently been discussed by Mr. R. D. Barnett in *Iraq*, 1935, p. 207. He suggests that the epic on the bowls is illustrated by the tale of Mot and Aleyin, recorded in the Shamra tablets.

one of the great Thalassocracies, which were convenient ways of expressing that the centre of gravity
of Mediterranean civilization had shifted from time
to time. For a generation immediately before the
rise of Phoenician power the Cypriots are said to
have ruled the Levant. Nothing is in fact more
probable, for Cyprus was almost the only place in
the east Mediterranean which had escaped the universal
ruin. Cyprus changed slowly under the new influences and received an Iron Age as well as the rest of
Greece, but it resembled the Iron Age only of north
Syria. As usual, Cyprus adapted universal conditions
to her own particular way of life. The usual iron
swords of Central European type make their appearance [1] and the usual drab background of Iron Age life
appears in the island. The memory of the Mycenaean
mode of life and taste lingers on in pottery and in
metal-work. Gold is not rare, though less common
than in the Mycenaean Age. But it is much commoner than silver and often of a darker colour than
Mycenaean gold.[2] This may perhaps indicate a
change of market and the formation of new trade
connexions, but it would be dangerous to base conclusions on such slim evidence. The gold jewellery of this Iron Age is by no means contemptible.
New styles and technique appear ; the ' granulated '
mode of goldwork is an almost exclusive method of
this time, rare earlier and later.

The knowledge of iron and its working soon

[1] *Cesnola Collection*, No. 4725. A sword classified as ' Naue
Type II ', the well-known Danubian type.
[2] Myres, *Cesnola Catalogue*, p. 379.

penetrated Cyprus, almost certainly from the same Anatolian hinterland which had supplied so many influences to the island. The Hittites were credited with a monopoly of the knowledge of iron-working and often with a monopoly of the iron itself, in the brief period after the discovery of the metal and the break up of the Hittite empire that followed soon after. Cappadocia was the great iron-working centre, and Cappadocia had always been in some sort of contact with south Anatolia and Cyprus. The half-legendary Chalybes carried on the industry into the historical age.

In Cyprus itself the iron-working areas which grew up, as knowledge of iron developed, were mainly at Tamassos and at Soloi. Brown iron ore of some richness is found in the pyritic masses in the igneous regions. Magnetite and specular haematite are also found on the northern slopes of Mavrovouni.[1] There was no need for the islanders to import the metal.

But the contrast between Cyprus and its neighbour Rhodes at this time is complete. In Cyprus, after the Mycenaean cities had degenerated and declined in wealth, as they were bound to do after the mainland of Greece and the whole of the Aegean had been cut off from them, Cypriots settled down to an existence of which it could at least be said that it was tolerably safe and settled. But in mainland Greece all was confusion. Mycenae, Tiryns, Orchomenos and Thebes had fallen in ruin and Crete was a home for raiders and looters. Rhodes was in the same region

[1] Storrs and O'Brien, *Handbook*, p. 253.

of catastrophe, and suffered from the intruders. Her
rich Mycenaean settlement was replaced by one of
powerful Dorians who left their imprint throughout
history on the Rhodians and their polity. But, as
in earlier times, an invisible barrier was drawn between
Rhodes and her neighbour Cyprus and there seems
to have been little trace of a Rhodian intrusion into
the eastern island. In historical times Cypriots still
spoke Arcadian and Achaean pre-Dorian Greek,
inherited from the original Greek settlement, while
Rhodians spoke the broadest Dorian dialect. The
connexion with Rhodes which existed in Mycenaean
times was irrevocably broken. Cyprus drew in on
herself. But she was by no means free from trouble.
She appears in the background of the Trojan war,
under a king Cinyras, whose name seems un-Hellenic,
as sympathetic to the Greeks, but non-participant.
The famous corselet which Cinyras presented to
Agamemnon was merely a substitute for active
service. Cinyras is the only king mentioned, but he
is not presumed as king of the whole island. In the
Odyssey we hear of King Dmetor of the royal Argive
house of Iasos, who may conceivably be a survivor
of those earlier kings who had come over with the
first colonization.[1] After the Trojan war a fresh
arrival of Achaean colonists seems to have taken place.
But here we depend wholly on legend and there is
no archaeological evidence to support the theory.
But we hear of Teukros founding Salamis, the
Arcadian Agapenor at New Paphos, and Agamemnon

[1] In opposition to Evans, who thinks that he subdued the island
at this time as a new arrival. *Scripta Minoa*, p. 75.

is said to have captured Amathus [1] and to have driven out Cinyras. These stories may reflect arrivals after the fall of Troy of Achaeans who found life unstable in Old Greece. If they arrived and stayed they chose wisely. But there is no archaeological indication of any new intrusion at this time. Yet survivals there must have been for a long time after survivals of Mycenaean life were rendered impossible in mainland Greece. The *Cypria* and their acknowledged composition in Cyprus suggest that the use and employment of bards and their epics survived in Cyprus during these years of poverty and confusion. Elsewhere, except perhaps in the Ionian Islands of the Adriatic, where a similar continuity of life from Mycenaean to Iron Age seems to have existed, the employments of bards and the demand for their songs was rendered more precarious by the poverty of the times and the lack of princes and their courts, wealthy enough and educated enough to enjoy the products of poets. Homeric lays probably generated and lived in Ithaka and to our certain knowledge were made in Cyprus. Cyprus perhaps afforded a happier breeding-ground for poets than any other place in the Mediterranean at this time, because of its relatively undisturbed life. Illiteracy had clearly increased, as our history of the Cypriot script has shown, but there was no catastrophe and, as I have suggested, the Achaean kingship seems to have preserved a continuity right through the gap of the Dark Ages, thus affording conditions which would encourage the growth and continuance of poetry. Of Kings of

[1] Engel, *Kypros*, i, 228 (Theopompos); Evans, op. cit., p. 75, n. 3.

Cyprus before the historical and classical period we
know of few.   But even a few is enough to justify
us in believing in the continuity of the social organization.   King Casos of Cyprus and King Cinyras could
have been contemporaries.   The former was, in
legend, responsible for the eastwards colonizing
venture at Amyke.   Cinyras was a contemporary of
Agamemnon and in communication with him.   Both
these events may belong to the closing years of the
Mycenaean prosperity, though Casos and his venture
may conceivably have been a generation earlier.   He
cannot be precisely dated, and since Ras Shamra
shows Cypriot influences from 1350 onwards, the
Casian venture may belong to any period after this
date.   The obscure Dmetor king of Cyprus of the
Odyssey seems rather to fall into the Raiding Age
at the close of the Mycenaean era.   Our bronze
sceptre from an Early Iron Age grave at Amathus
(see above, p. 65), while not found with objects
which suggest a burial more or less royal than any
other at Amathus of this period, seems at least to
show that regalia were still in use and the kingship,
if only a name, at least remembered.

The growth of the *Cypria* took place, if not actually
in the Dark Ages then, like many of the elements and
sources of the Iliad,[1] at the court of Mycenae or some
other Mycenaean centre, before the catastrophe.   I do
not propose to beg more literary questions than are
required in this hypothesis ; nor is the title of the
Cypria even a proof that the poems were written in

[1] Nilsson, *Homer and Mycenae* 32 *and* 42, summarizing and
criticizing the views of Drerup.

Cyprus. But one of the various candidates for authorship is a certain Stasinos [1] whose name is Cypriot. There was a Stasanor of Soloi, [2] two kings Stasioikos of Marion, [3] a king Stasandros of Paphos [4] and the name Stasicrates occurs on a Cypriot inscription in the Classical script, and there is in the Cesnola Collection a Cypriot statue of one Stasidamos. [5] Names with this prefix thus seem to be peculiarly popular in Cyprus.

One indication of continuity between the Bronze Age and the Iron Age may be found at a site recently excavated by the Swedish Expedition, known as Aghios Jakovos, on the foothills of the Kerynia Mountains due north of Enkomi. The foundations of a rectangular sanctuary were found, measuring 6·95 × 10·75m. This building bears a resemblance to a primitive Greek temple and is not unlike the seventh- or eighth-century temples of Prinias and Dreros in proportions and plan. But it would be premature to classify it definitely as a temple. The building was not actually built over the earlier Bronze Age sanctuary, but it was quite close to it and seems to have superseded it. The date given by the excavators to the building is that of 'Cypro-Geometric III', that is to say, a fairly advanced stage of the Iron Age. But there are elements datable at periods that go back through the previous Iron Age periods to the close of the Bronze Age. The 'temple' has a primitive pronaos and seems to have been roofed;

[1] Athenaeus, 682 D.   [2] Strabo, xiv, 6.3.
[3] Hill, *Cat. Coins of Cyprus*, p. lvii, and Diodorus, xix, 62.
[4] Hill, op. cit., p. lxix.   [5] Myres, *Catalogue*, p. 317.

its first period of construction seems to have been nearer the beginning of the Iron Age.

Hitherto no satisfactory excavation has been carried out on a habitation-site where levels of the Bronze Age and of the Iron Age have been found in order of deposit. Until such a site has been excavated the chronology of the Bronze and Iron Ages must remain uncertain. The date usually assigned to the close of the Bronze Age is 1000 B.C. At present we have no precision at all and this is hardly more than a convenient guess. It is generally believed that the Bronze Age continued for at least a century after it had perished in mainland Greece and the Aegean. Gjerstad has no further modification of this date to offer and gives it in his *Studies on Prehistoric Cyprus*,[1] published in 1926.

Mr. Wainwright has recently[2] made a complete and convincing study of the origin of iron and iron-working, and comes to the conclusion that iron was widely known in Asia Minor before the fourteenth century B.C. and exported after that date freely to neighbouring lands. Yet the general use of iron came very slowly and he sees no reason to alter the date of the first appearance of iron in Cyprus, which occurs at the close of the last Mycenaean period in the island and generally in the Greek world about 1100 B.C. Yet the fact that the main iron-producing areas of Kissuwadna[3] and Tabal were not far inland

---

[1] p. 335. At St. Jakovos continuity between Bronze and Iron Age is indicated. *S.C.E.*, I, p. 368.
[2] *Antiquity*, 1936, p. 1, 'The coming of Iron'.
[3] See Schachermeyer, op. cit., p. 87.

from the head of the Gulf of Alexandretta and within
easy reach of Cyprus, whose islanders could see the
neighbouring shores from their north coast, does not
seem in any way to have speeded up an iron age in
Cyprus. The curious fact remains that Cyprus
received the general use of iron, if anything, a little
later than the rest of the Greek world. The only
explanation of this must be the invincible conservatism
of the Cypriots, who, like the Egyptians, preferred
to remain in an age of bronze when the fashionable
metal was spreading far and wide in the world round
them. For Egypt was the last country to accept an
iron age in the Aegean and Levant.[1]

[1] Wainwright, op. cit. ; Lucas, op. cit., p. 406. The Egyptians were not in a full iron age until about 700 B.C.

CHAPTER VI

THE KINGDOMS OF CYPRUS

σκηπτοῦχοι βασιλῆες

IT is difficult, if not impossible, to prove a continuity between the Achaean kingdoms of Cyprus and those of the Classical period. But there is every indication short of actual scientific proof that such continuity did in fact exist. The earliest list of names of Cypriot cities occurs in the temple-inscription at Medinet Habu in Egypt, where eight names are given (see above, p. 130). The correspondence with Cypriot city-names is so close that it would be unwise to disregard this inscription as being inapplicable to Cyprus on the grounds of the uncertainty of place-name parallels. The list gives us Salamis, Soloi, Kition, Marion, Idalion, and Kurion, all well-known places, and also Akamas and Kerynia. The last two (Kerynia in the inscription appears as Kerena and Kir . . .), even if they presuppose cities of very small importance, hardly known as large places to later history, do not necessarily invalidate the general assumption that the inscription refers to Cyprus.

The next external reference to Cypriot cities and their kings is in the year 707 B.C., when Cyprus was subjugated by the Assyrians under Sargon. The

PLATE IX

THE NORTHERN MOUNTAIN RIDGE, LOOKING SOUTH-WEST, ON THE KYRENIA-KARAVAS ROAD

famous stele at Berlin[1] mentions seven kings in all
in the island, though this need not be taken to mean
that there were no more than seven, any more than
that the mention of the ' King of Alasia ' who writes
to Amenhotep III should be taken to imply that there
was then only one king of Cyprus.[2] It does, however,
allow us to assume the existence for certain of the
institution of the kingship in the island in the Bronze
Age, for which we have already examined the other
evidence.

The Berlin document is inscribed on a column,
found in 1845 on the Bamboula site at Kition. The
column is made of local stone and was almost
certainly carved on the spot. It records the homage
and tribute of

> the seven kings of the region of Yah, a district of the land
> of Atnana who dwell a distance of seven days' journey in the
> western sea, the name of whose land is from ancient times. . . .
> Fear seizes them : they brought to me (vessels of) KAL wood and
> KU wood, the treasures of their land, to Babylon, and they
> kissed my feet. In those days I had a table of stone set up . . .

Later still in the reign of Sennacherib, son of Sargon,
comes a record from Kuyundjik in which it is said
that Elulaeus, king of Sidon, ' fled from the midst of
the western land away to the island of Yaatnana in
mid-sea '.[3]

Most explicit of all is the record of the ten Cypriot

[1] Oberhummer, *Cypern*, p. 8.
[2] This Cypriot king writes to his Egyptian confrère, to explain
that the copper-working of Alasia has temporarily ceased. See
Hall, *B.S.A.*, viii, 168.
[3] Oberhummer, p. 10.

kings whose names and cities are recorded on a partly
broken cylinder in the British Museum. It belongs
to the time of Esarhaddon and Assurbanipal (681–626),
the Sargonids. The significant fact about this list
is that the names of the kings are, if the transliteration
from the Assyrian forms is correct, mainly Greek.
We find the list of names as follows :

> Ikiistura of Idi(li) or Edihaal
> Pilaaguraa of Kiitrusi
> Kiisu of Siluua
> Ituuandaar of Paapa
> Irisu of Siillu
> Damasu of Kurii
> Rumisu of Tamisu
> Damausu of Kartihadaasti
> Unasagusu of Lidiir
> Pususu of Nurii.

The rubric at the end of the inscription states that
there were in all the subjugated regions here recorded

> ten kings of the land of Yatnana in the middle of the sea : in
> all, 22 kings of the land of the Hatti on the sea coast and in
> the middle of the sea.[1]

Of the ten kings all are described as ' king of the land
of' except the first Ikiistura, who is ' king of the city
of'.

The Graecized names where they can be Graecized
are as follows, with the Greek forms of their kingdoms :

[1] Oberhummer, p. 15.

Ikistura of Idalion
Pylagoras of Khytroi
Kiisu of Salamis
Eteander of Paphos
Irisu of Soloi
Damasu of Kurion
Rumisu of Tamassos
Damasu of Kartihadasti = 'New City' = Carthage = probably Kition.
Onesagoras of Ledron (or Ledroi or Ledrai, a late Greek name for the predecessor of Nicosia).
Pususu of Nurii (possibly Urania, but better unidentified).

A comparison of this list with the only other list, that of the Medinet Habu inscription, shows that the kingdoms of Idalion, Kurion, Soloi, Kition and Salamis had survived as kingdoms from the thirteenth to the seventh centuries. On the other hand, the kingdoms of Marion, Akamas and Kerynia, mentioned in the Egyptian list, have vanished, while Khytroi, Paphos, Tamassos, Ledron and 'Nurii' appear as new kingdoms, or at least as new names. It would, however, be unwise to assume that any omission in either list presupposes that the kingdom did not exist at the time of the inscription, the more so since in the later list Tamassos-Temese and Paphos are cities which have at least the guarantee for an existence in the Homeric poems, and have provided archaeological evidence to show that they were inhabited in Mycenaean times at the latest. Probably the capital of a given kingdom shifted from age to age, kingdoms were reformed and their boundaries reshaped. But we are left with several small and problematical kingdoms represented by the names Akamas and Kerynia in the Egyptian list, and Khytroi, Ledron and ' Nurii' in the Assyrian for which we have no archaeological, historical or numismatic background whatever. They must be pigeon-holed as kingdoms for which we must await the results of further archaeological research.

It is interesting to compare these lists with the total of nine cities [1] for the fourth century—Salamis, Paphos, Soloi, Kurion, Kition, Lapethos, Kerynia, Marion and Amathus.

Of these Amathus and Lapethos appear for the first time in written records, while Kerynia reappears from its obscurity since the Bronze Age, together with Marion, while Idalion, common to both the earlier lists, vanishes. Tamassos, a famous ancient city, appears only in the Assyrian list.

It is interesting to compare this literary evidence with the more solid information of coinage. Certain attributions of series of coins have been made for Kition, Idalion, Lapethos, Marion, Paphos and Salamis. Conjectural attributions have been made for Golgoi and for Amathus, and, in the early period, for Lapethos. The first city to strike coins, as one might expect in view of the fact that it appears in the Egyptian, the Assyrian and in the fourth-century lists and has an assured continuity historically and archaeologically, is Salamis. The earliest issues are those of Euelthon, whose date is approximately 530–520, a king known to Herodotus.[2] They bear his name in

---

[1] Diodorus, xvi, 42.   [2] IV, 162.

PLATE X

LAPETHOS

the Cypriot script, thus giving us one of the earliest preserved instances of the Classical script. But there are no other certain city-issues for the sixth century. The coinage of Kition falls about 500 B.C. and that of Idalion and Paphos to the first half of the fifth century. A conjectural attribution of coins to Golgoi and another for Amathus would allow us to assume that those cities issued their first coins in the middle of the fifth century. The earliest coins of Marion fall into the second half or middle of the fifth century. There is no certain attribution of coins to Lapethos except for the years 313–312 B.C.,[1] though a series is tentatively assigned to the city for the first half of the fifth century. A similar doubtful attribution also makes it possible that coins were issued by Soloi in the early fifth century.

From this numismatic evidence it appears at least that Salamis was the most important city of the island and that there were certainly kings of Salamis from the beginning to the end of its independent existence. There are also names of kings preserved on the coinage of Kition, Idalion, Lapethos (for the fourth century only),[2] Marion and Paphos, while there is historical record of the names of kings of Soloi. The numismatic list thus corresponds fairly closely with the list of nine kingdoms given by Diodorus Siculus. The only cities known in the fourth century B.C. and unrepresented by any coinage are Kerynia and Kurion. The last named is a most remarkable lacuna. There

[1] B.M.C., *Cyprus*, p. liii.
[2] B.M.C., *Cyprus*, p. 30. A possible Phoenician king called Sidqmelek.

II

are no coins which can safely be given to this kingdom. Those attributed by Babelon to Kurion are now generally accepted as belonging to Marion. Coins are attributed to Golgoi and Idalion, but the attribution to Golgoi is not certain. On the other hand, the name of king Kara . . . is inscribed on coins of Idalion as well as of a king Ki . . . ⧺ ⩜ ,[1] both names being impossible to complete owing to the abbreviation in the script. This enigmatical name of King Kara . . . (⧺ ⇑ ⵖ) has recently been re-read as Arkalos, an Argive name which suits the Argive traditions of Idalion. But Hill[2] rightly points out that the syllable Ra cannot conceivably be read as Ar. But we are left with an alternative to Kara of Raka . . . which is not impossible. Names derivative from ῥάξ are conceivable.

The omission of Kerynia from the fourth-century list may be due to its insignificance at all periods, and the omission of Idalion may be due to the fact, noted by Hill,[3] that the city seems to have enjoyed a more democratic form of government than others in the island, if one can safely infer this from the use of the name of the place or its inhabitants recorded in the inscription on one type of Idalian coin where one would expect the name of a king, and the fixing of

[1] B.M.C., Cyprus, p. 26, n. 8. And E. S. G. Robinson, Num. Chron., xv, 5th series, p. 181.

[2] Idem, p. 26. Re-read by Dikaios in Num. Chron., xv, 5th series, No. 60, pp. 282–4. He reads the script inscription from right to left, reversing the order of the reading which produced βα.κα.ρα, thus geting αρ.κα.βα = ᾿Αρκαλου βασιλεως. Hill refutes this reading in Num. Chron., No. 61, p. 88.

[3] B.M.C., Cyprus, p. l.

a date in Idalian history in the famous Dali bronze
tablet by the name of an eponymous magistrate
instead of by a regnal year. Idalion also was finally
conquered by Kition in the middle of the fifth century
and so would have little claim to be known as an
independent city if, by then, Kition and Idalion were
one kingdom with Kition as predominant partner.

The combined evidence of these three lists, the
Egyptian, Assyrian and that provided by the coinage
evidence, together with the mention of the seven
kings in the time of Sargon, justifies at least the assumption that the kingship in Cyprus was a long-standing
political state-system which lasted from Achaean to
Ptolemaic times. That it deeply interested the democratic Greeks of the mainland is indicated by the fact
that Theophrastos wrote a work entitled *The Kingdoms
of the Cypriots*. The latest description of a Cypriot
king is preserved in Athenaeus in a fragment quoted
from a comedy by Antiphanes.[1] Here the king of
Paphos is described as sitting at dinner with an
elaborate equivalent of the *punkah* to cool him. He
was anointed with Tyrian oil made from a fruit to
which the doves flying round the room were notori-
ously addicted. As the doves approached his head
they were driven off by attendants so that the king
was kept cool by the constant fluttering of their wings.
It is easy to recognize here the satire of a sophisticated
Greek and some perversion of the truth. But it
suggests an account which travellers' gossip had
suggested. The existence of kings and doves at

[1] VI, 257.

Paphos was sufficient to produce a humorous con-
flation.

It remains to see how far archaeological research
has thrown any light on the Cypriot kingship.

The recent excavations of the Swedish Mission have,
among other sites, been carried out at Marion, Idalion
and Amathus.[1] These are indeed the first systematic
and scientific excavations at these sites, which have
been largely damaged by uncontrolled or unsystematic
excavations. Marion was first excavated in 1885 by
Ohnefalsch-Richter and again in 1886 by him on
behalf of three Englishmen. Four hundred and forty-
one tombs were opened during these researches and the
resulting collection was sold by auction at Paris in
1887, with the exception of a few pieces given to the
British Museum and one third which went to the
Cyprus government.[2] In 1889 and 1890 further
excavations of a more methodical nature were carried
out by the Cyprus Excavation Fund.[3] The Swedish
excavators dug ninety-eight tombs covering a period
from Geometric times to late Classical. They came
to the conclusion that, disregarding a dispute which
had raged unconclusively,[4] the site of Marion is
actually the modern πόλις τῆς Χρυσοχοῦ. They
think that the promontory of Pyrgos is the ancient
Kallinousa and is the natural boundary between the

[1] S.C.E., II, pp. 1, 181, 460.

[2] The excavations were published in Berlin in 1888, *Das
Gräberfeld von Marion*, by P. Hermann. See Myres, *Cyprus Cat.*,
p. 9. See also *J.H.S.*, x, p. 281.

[3] For references see Myres, loc. cit.

[4] S.C.E., II, p. 182 ff.

kingdoms of Soloi and Marion. They accept the identifications of Oberhummer's map. The later town of Arsinoe is in the plain and the excavators think that it covers the site of the late Archaic and Classical city. Their finds in detail do not help to illuminate the history of the kingdom, beyond showing that it preserved a continuity from at least the beginning of the Iron Age.

If Marion is really represented by the Aimar of the Medinet Habu inscription, it is perhaps surprising that we do not hear of it in the Esarhaddon list. But here we can check the facts by archaeological evidence and demonstrate that a city on the site, presumably of the same name, existed from at least 800 B.C., to judge by the large quantities of Early Iron Age pottery found in all excavations, and that that city existed continuously through the period covered by the Assyrian domination.

Of the shape and disposition of this city we know nothing, since only necropoleis have been excavated in all the excavations. Marion, in the opinion of Myres, was 'the headquarters of the copper trade with the West'.[1] Ancient copper mines, largely exhausted, exist in the hills of the hinterland at Tylliria, and larger quantities of imported Hellenic pottery have been found at Marion than at other sites.

No history of the kingdom is recorded before 449 when it was captured by Kimon.[2] Strabo[3] mentions

[1] Cyprus Museum Catalogue, p. 9.
[2] Hill, B.M.C. Cat., Cyprus, p. lvii (an emendation of Diodorus, xii, 3.3.).   [3] XIV, 6.3.

that there was a grove of Zeus, and from a sixth-
century inscription [1] we learn of a cult of Phersephatta-
Persephone. On the coins the names of two kings,
Stasioikos and Timocharis, occur. The former is a
predecessor of the Stasioikos who in 315 sided with
Ptolemy.

The site of Idalion was also excavated by the
Swedish Mission.[2] These excavations verified the
conclusions previously established by Lang and Ohnefalsch-Richter that the site—which covers a sharp
outcrop of limestone from the plain—consisted of two
acropoleis situated on two separate hillocks. The
western of the two acropoleis was in the Bronze Age
a fortified stronghold—clear proof that Idalion had a
history as a town at a date earlier even than that of the
Medinet Habu inscription. Later this stronghold was
occupied in Classical times as a sanctuary of Anaït-
Athena. On a terrace below the summit of this
acropolis and below the sanctuary were found the
foundations of a royal palace, or at least of a structure
which the excavators identify as such. On the summit of the eastern acropolis was a sanctuary of Aphrodite. Between the two acropoleis was a sanctuary of
Reseph-Apollo, situated in the dip between the two
hills. The lower town was on the plain surrounded by
walls, and the necropolis was situated outside these
walls and also on the hillside south of the twin acropoleis. Most of these buildings and the main outlines
of the walls had been established in previous excavations. Of these the most important were made by

[1] *J.H.S.*, xi, 74.
[2] Op. cit., p. 461 ff., and Plans IV and V.

Ohnefalsch-Richter in 1883 and by Dümmler in 1885, but no systematic publication followed. The site had been extensively looted at an earlier date, and one of the most important discoveries made during this looting was of the silver paterae, now in the Louvre, and of the famous bronze tablet acquired by the Duc de Luynes. We hear from the coinage of only one Idalian king, Stasicypros, the last king before the capture of the city by Kition.

The coins attributed to Idalion have as a principal symbol the lotus-flower. Whether this can be taken as indicating the local cult of Aphrodite-Astarte, as Hill thinks,[1] is largely a matter of conjecture. Probably this Egyptian motif is merely one of the many such patterns which caught the fancy of Cypriots in the sixth century, when a wealth of Oriental designs of different kinds flooded the island and lasted well into the decorative repertoire of the fifth century.

The large quantity of sculptures found at Idalion in earlier excavations are mainly at Berlin and in the Nicosia Museum.

The site of Amathus was the third city to be excavated by the Swedish Mission. The site is clearly marked, on a bluff that rises steeply from the sea. The walls and harbour works are traceable. In 1893–4 three hundred tombs were opened by contract for the British Museum, the work being carefully supervised by Smith and Myres.

The results of the Swedish excavations of 1930 confirmed the general conclusions stated above, that the city had no Bronze Age history. The earliest

[1] B.M.C. Cat., Cyprus, p. 1.

recorded tombs are of the Geometric Age.[1] No
pottery of the Mycenaean period has ever been found
at Amathus.

But Amathus is remarkable for its ashlar-built
tombs of the Archaic period. Those described by
Cesnola as having been excavated by him are extant
and their plans have now been accurately drawn.[2]
Two further tombs of the same magnificent ashlar was
opened by the Swedish excavators in 1930. But both
had been previously robbed. In plan and elevation
they correspond with the main types of the Cesnola
tombs, and also with the recently opened tomb at
Pyla.[3]

This account of the kingship, however sketchy,
would not be complete without mention of one of
the major works of art in Cyprus, the superb gold-
and-enamel sceptre in the Nicosia Museum. If any
object can claim to be royal it is this. It reached the
Museum via the Customs, whose officers had removed
it from the luggage of a would-be emigrant. It
languished in the Customs House at Larnaka for some
years before it reached its final destination. It has
only recently been published [4] (Plate XI).

Its temporary owner told the story that it was
found by a peasant digging in a field near Episkopi,

[1] The Chariot crater said by Cesnola, *Cyprus*, p. 268, to have
been found here, certainly comes from elsewhere. *S.C.E.*, vol.
ii, p. 2.

[2] *S.C.E.*, ii, text, Fig. 47.

[3] Dikaios, *Dept. of Antiquities Report*, 1934, p. 9, and see below,
p. 203.

[4] Dudley-Buxton, Casson and Myres in *Man.*, 1932, p. 1–3.

PLATE XI

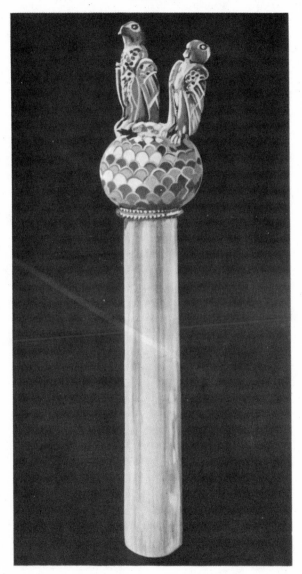

GOLD AND ENAMELLED SCEPTRE
SAID TO COME FROM KURION
(*Nicosia Museum*)

not far from the site of Kurion.[1] Its date is problematic, but there seems some consensus of opinion that it is of the late seventh or early sixth century. If, indeed, it comes from ancient Kurion, then there is every reason to think that it is part of the royal regalia of that kingdom.

As a work of art it is unique. Nothing resembling it is known in the archaic Greek world. On the other hand, nothing about it is un-Hellenic. That it is a sceptre there is no doubt at all. Its gold tube is thin and hollow, evidently for mounting on a wooden or ivory handle. The work is delicate and fine and the enamel amazingly preserved. The scale-pattern of the bulb recalls the scale-patterns on Corinthian pottery as well as the scale-garment over the shoulders of the Auxerre Cretan statue in the Louvre which belongs to the late seventh century. That birds on a sceptre have a royal connotation, is evident from the *Birds* of Aristophanes.[2]

The fact that parallels are hard to find in the Greek world is not to be counted against the Hellenic claims of this sceptre, for there were few kings outside Cyprus among Hellenic peoples.

That it belongs to the Bronze Age kingdom of Kurion is unlikely, for the enamel-work and the scale ornament are both typical of archaic Greek work.

---

[1] On a visit to Episkopi in 1935 I was assured that the belief was current in the village that it had, in fact, been found there.

[2] 1. 508.

ἦρχον δ' οὕτω σφόδρα τὴν ἀρχήν, ὥστ' εἰ τις καὶ βασιλεύοι ἐν ταῖς πόλεσιν τῶν Ἑλλήνων Ἀγαμέμνων ἢ Μενέλαος ἐπὶ τῶν σκήπτρων ἐκάθητ' ὄρνις μετέχων ὅ τι δωροδοκοίη.

CHAPTER VII

CYPRIOT ART

THE *Κύπριος χαρακτήρ* which evidently impressed the mainland Greeks may be generally interpreted as a quality which concerned both appearance and behaviour. It has already been evident from the Early Bronze Age that whatever influences reached Cyprus from outside, the Cypriots themselves always modified those influences into forms which could never be confused with or identifiable as the originals. Even when the almost overpowering Mycenaean fashions swept the board and native Cypriot designs and taste were largely subordinated, and confined to a few specific types of works of art and industry, there rapidly appeared in the purest Mycenaean types of pottery certain tendencies which we have seen to be peculiar to the island. These tendencies may not to any large extent reflect anything that had gone before in Cypriot ceramic history, yet they indicate a certain insular preference for shapes and designs which is not found outside Cyprus.

The later history of Cypriot artistic production resembles the earlier. The dull and uneventful twilight of the Early Iron Age, not so poverty-stricken as in many parts of mainland Greece but less enterprising, still showed the Cypriot potter and maker of small artistic objects clinging to fashions which he had himself invented or modified, with a persistence and dullness almost unequalled in antiquity in Greek lands. The passion for compass-drawn concentric circles and for circles round necks and bodies which show little feeling for rhythm and none for grace, stamp the Geometric period of Cypriot art as almost entirely devoid of invention, compared with some of the intensely experimental and thoughtful Geometric work of the mainland. And yet throughout the Cypriot Geometric period there is a quality which stamps all work as Cypriot. No one could ever mistake a Cypriot Geometric vase for the work of any other Greek region. Their Cypriot character is clearly written on them. And the inference is simple enough —that in the Early Iron Age the Cypriot artists had sunk into a slough of utter dullness. Out of touch with their compatriots, surrounded by a little-used sea —for trade and traffic immediately after the fall of the Mycenaean world must have sunk to very small proportions—they were left to vegetate. Their nearest neighbour, Rhodes, was, as in all periods before the Mycenaean, and in almost all periods later, separated from them by an invisible barrier, the cause and origin of which is remarkably obscure. Anatolia was in chaos after the invasions which had finally disrupted the Hittite empire, and Syria was no longer a rich land for Mycenaean and Egyptian exploitation. What exactly was the duration of this long and dull Geometric period is not yet certainly fixed. But it comes to a close with the same suddenness and for the same reasons as did the Geometric period in the rest of

Greece. What happened to the rest of Greece happened to Cyprus. The long period of trial and experiment in Geometric Greece that, in the end, seemed to lead nowhere was magically transformed into a world of rich variety and endless imagination by the first contact of mainland Greeks with Oriental ideas. They had at last found a stimulant, they had found forms and designs and colours which excited them, but which excited them not to mere emulation and simple copying, but to the creation of new syntheses which, in their intention as in our estimation, transcended the original inspiration. The Orientalizing period of Greek art is the most interesting of all periods precisely because it shows us exactly how the Greek mind and intelligence reacted to stimulants, how, excited by the rich and frequently jaded art of Oriental peoples, the Greek, perhaps sometimes unconsciously, imparted to those prototypes qualities which their creators had never conceived. And so the Orientalizing period of Greek art is the most absorbing, if only because we see the very young pupil almost at his first lesson outstripping his master.

Now the Cypriot artist was no stranger to Oriental art. For centuries artists had lived in a world where Assyrian, Hittite, and Egyptian art was fully known and widely admired. True, no alien artist had actually been admitted into the island except the maker of Sargon stele, which was apparently made at Kition. Unless future excavation reveals examples, we can with some assurance assume that no first-class Assyrian or Hittite sculpture was ever made by Assyrians or Hittites in Cyprus. Even authentic Egyptian monuments are almost completely absent, despite the Egyptian control of Cyprus under Amasis, and, later, the succeeding Persian ownership of Cyprus, from 525 B.C. down to Alexander the Great, introduced no Persian architecture or sculpture and only minor works of art to the island. Yet all the Oriental modes of art, from period to period, were well enough known to Cypriots : but with an unusually insular self-protection they excluded them, absorbing only their influence, and that from afar. The complete absence of standard types of Mycenaean architecture from Cyprus is another indication of the lack of will or desire on the part of Cypriots to absorb another culture completely.

And so, when the rest of the Greek world welcomed these Oriental influences and, by travel and trade, learnt Oriental repertoires and were inspired by them, the Cypriots, long accustomed to this Orient, turned with less excitement and less zeal towards the new vogues and fashions.

I am not suggesting that Cypriot artists were by nature either stupid and inartistic, or incompetent and jaded. They were neither. But they were an ancient stock. The Greek element in the island, which by the eighth century was the predominant element and probably the largest part of the population, had, after all, probably arrived in the Bronze Age, if the hypothesis that the Mycenaean colonists were Greek by race is acceptable. Since their arrival there had been no influx of fresh Greeks, except perhaps for possible arrivals of stray settlers about the time of the fall of Troy, and the great Dorian invasion that flowed as far south-east as Rhodes, there stopped. Cypriots remained as firmly Achaean in language and, probably also in mode of life and behaviour, in the fourth as in the fourteenth or thirteenth century. Dorian dialect and Dorian architecture are completely absent; there was no Achaean architecture to offer as an alternative, and so the Cypriots were never tempted to build a single Dorian temple in their island. Indeed, Greek temples as such, even of Ionian types, are not to be found at all, and here again we meet that stubborn conservatism of Cypriots. The great temple at Paphos was architecturally *sui generis*, until Roman times. Whatever else the essentially Greek Cypriots made that was Greek, they did not make Greek buildings. It is this absence of temples and other buildings of the known Greek types that makes archaeologists so often assume that Cyprus was a very un-Greek island and steeped in the fashions and habits of the Orient. Yet no conclusion can be more unjust or more inaccurate. The only correct conclusion that can be drawn is that the Cypriots were not an architecturally-minded folk and that when they established contact with another culture or with other forms of Greek culture they simply were not interested in the architectural achievements of those cultures. They rejected alike Mycenaean, Assyrian, Hittite, Egyptian and Persian architectural conceptions and when they built for themselves, as they did at Vouni and at Paphos, where we can study adequately the remains of a Cypriot palace and a Cypriot temple, they built in a manner entirely their own. The very fact that controversies have raged so long about the Oriental affinities of these two build-

PLATE XII

COURTYARD OF THE PALACE AT VOUNI
THE ATRIUM AND ATHENA-PEDESTAL ARE SEEN IN THE BACKGROUND

ings [1] is adequate proof that their Oriental origin is not
patent and obvious. True enough, neither building
is Greek, but it is equally true that neither is a mere
synthesis or pastiche of Oriental motives.

It is this stubbornness of the Cypriot artist and
architect and this lack of youthful enthusiasm which
distinguishes Cyprus at the period of Oriental influence. Cyprus was by then an old Greek world,
uninvigorated by Dorian intrusions, with a background
of autochthonous Cypriots of non-Greek habits, the
descendants of the Anatolians of the Bronze Age.
These pre-Achaean Cypriots, who were, as far as we
can tell, neither of Greek blood nor of Greek language,
seem to have persisted to the end and largely to have
reinforced the insular and ' nationalistic ' characteristics
of Cypriot history and art. It is to them that we can,
perhaps, attribute the ' nationalistic ' tendency which
sought to preserve the ancient syllabary [2] and to use
it as a rival to the newfangled Greek characters. No
doubt the Achaean section of the population was just
as eager to preserve and emphasize what they had
themselves originally introduced from the mainland
to the island (see above, p. 67). But their conservatism would have been emphasized by the con-

[1] Gjerstad and V. Muller in *A.J.A.* 36, p. 409 and 37, pp. 589
and 658. C. Blinkenberg, *Le Temple de Paphos, Copenhagen,*
1924. Blinkenberg and others see in the temple at Paphos a
clearly Minoan plan and elevation. But the comparison with
Minoan architecture is only apposite when the Paphian temple
is compared with the small gold shrine from Mycenae found
in the third Shaft Grave. We have no proof that this model
of a shrine is not of the shrine at Paphos.

[2] See above, p. 96.

servatism of the older stock. Certainly to the older
stock can be attributed the preservation of the non-
Greek language which was spoken down to the fourth
century and is preserved in the famous inscriptions of
the Louvre, of the Ashmolean and in other instances.[1]

Here was set a stage totally different from that prepared in Greece proper. And a comparison of the
way in which Cypriot artists reacted to the direct
approach of Oriental influences, with the same reaction
of other Greeks, is a comparison fertile in useful inferences for those who wish to study the interaction
of Occident and Orient.

The Oriental influences came to Cyprus direct and
with full impact. Greek influences came indirectly,
but, because the Cypriots were in the main of Greek
blood, with a larger appeal and with more stimulative
power. I propose here to study Cypriot art as a whole
and not to divide it into ceramic, sculpture and the
minor arts and crafts. Taken as a whole we can see
the Oriental influences approaching it as a whole,
being absorbed, rejected and replaced. Only one
branch of art seems to stand quite apart—the art of
the coinage of Cyprus. Cypriot coins in style have
little, if any, contact with Cypriot artistic styles. They
bear a close relation to the art of eastern Greece and the
islands and not to Cyprus. This paradox can probably
be explained by assuming that coin-dies were made
by die-cutters from outside Cyprus. The coin-art of
the island must therefore be considered separately.

Pottery-designs and sculpture will be here taken as
two modes of art which absorb in the same way the

[1] F. Bork, *Die Sprache von Alasija*, 1930.

various and successive Oriental influences. Other artistic activities are so slight and so occasional that they hardly contribute to our particular study. There seems to have been no Cypriot mural or tomb painting —at least none has survived—and Cypriot bronzework is rare. On the other hand, the amount of Cypriot pottery and sculpture available for study is enormous. The Cypriot tradition, inherited from the Early Bronze Age, of burying their dead, richly equipped with pottery vessels, in deeply cut rock-tombs, like family vaults, has led to the preservation of immense quantities of pots at all periods. The less elaborate tombs of Greece proper, and the inability of their makers to hide them as efficiently as did the Cypriots, has deprived us of much mainland and island Greek pottery. Rock-tombs were never popular in the Greek mainland ; in Cyprus they were universal throughout Cypriot history.

So with sculpture. The only materials available for sculpture were alluvial clay and soft limestone. The unlimited supply of both these materials and the ease with which they could be worked has led to the survival of quantities of sculpture almost as immense in proportion as the quantities of pottery. The various types of Cypriot limestone range in colour from dark golden yellow to almost dead white and all are soft enough to be cut with a knife. The knife is, indeed, one of the commonest of the Cypriot sculptor's tools. This softness of material clearly implies that the preliminary work on the making of a statue would be quick and light. The sculptor could save much time compared with the sculptor of Pentelic or Parian

12

marble. Not only would he save time in the preliminary work but also in the work of actual execution.
That, partly, explains the fact that so many examples
of Cypriot sculpture survive. But, curiously enough,
Cypriot sculpture is nearly always sculpture in the
round or of unifacial figures completely detached from
a background. Reliefs are extremely rare and only
occasionally successful. Even very low relief, for
which soft limestone is excellently suited, never becomes popular. This partiality for sculpture in the
round is mainly due to the fact that when sculpture
started in Cyprus the prototypes that inspired work
were the massive sculptures of Egyptian art and of the
earliest periods of Greek island sculpture. The local
stone was easily workable and this also was a contributing factor. The novice was trained at the outset in a world where sculpture in the round was
predominant. Conservative as always, the Cypriot
artists stuck to their early preferences.

The development of Cypriot sculpture is, as in most
parts of the Greek world, controlled by political
events. What happened to Cyprus happened also to
its art. The purely Geometric period of Greek
ceramic design is generally held to have lasted from
1000 to 700 B.C.[1] This phase of design in Cyprus
has been given, until recently, the misnomer of Greco-
Phoenician. This term presumed that Cyprus at this
time was subject to alternating Greek and Phoenician
enterprise and that it was constantly shifting its
allegiance from one side to the other. But this corresponds to no known historical facts and the Phoenicians

[1] Myres, *Cesnola Collection*, p. 62.

do not seem to have settled in the island or to have
counted as an element of the population of importance
until the late eighth century at the earliest. Even then
their interests were strictly localized, mainly in Kition
and Idalion.

What happens to this Geometric style is that it
gradually changes, by slow steps from a strict geometry
of decoration to a rich and imaginative efflorescence of
pattern, undoubtedly Oriental in its elements, certainly
Cypriot in conception. This change took place between 700 and 600 and culminated in an astonishing
pictorial style which stands out as one of the great
Cypriot contributions to ceramic design. While
shapes of pots never attain the grace of mainland types
the designs are brilliant. Their exotic quality and
passionate rhythms stamp them as creations quite
peculiar to a certain period and a certain people.
Apparently Oriental at first glance, they slowly reveal
qualities essentially Greek. But they also reveal one
quality which is essentially Cypriot. It has been
observed [1] that throughout Cypriot ceramic history
Cypriot painters repeatedly struggle against convention.

Every now and then the painter makes either a hope-
less attempt at free drawing which is as puerile as it is
ridiculous,[2] but every now and then he succeeds in
producing a real masterpiece of individual draughtsmanship which conforms to no known style or
manner. Even in the highly conventionalized Myce-

[1] See Myres in *Essays on Aegean Archaeology*, 1927, p. 72 ff.
[2] *Cesnola Collection*, No. 513, painting on a clay tripod. *B.M.
Cat. Vases*, I, ii, Nos. C. 737 and C. 736.

naean Age the Cypriot Mycenaean painter sometimes makes this attempt at free drawing.[1] Indeed, the general quality which distinguishes Cypriot Mycenaean scenic vases from other Mycenaean decoration is its vitality and easy draughtsmanship. The tendency which reappears in the Orientalizing period may well be a long-standing characteristic of Cypriot artists.

The best examples of this emancipated style are seen in the bird-vases, which with their narrow necks and globular bodies preserve the ancestral gourd-shape so popular in Cyprus in every period. On these vases we see one single device, a flying, running or standing bird. The bird is so spaced and drawn that it satisfies completely the desire of the decorator to adorn the vase. He therefore is not frequently tempted, as were so many Geometric artists, to add filling ornament. The fact that he did not is testimony enough to his good taste, and the drawing of the birds, in most cases, is swift and artistic.[2] The Oriental origin of these bird types is certain. The inspiration behind them is to be identified as the royal hawks and vultures of Egyptian painting and jewellery. Probably the latter, in the form of portable works of art, gave the Cypriot artist

---

[1] *B.M. Cat. Vases*, I, ii, No. C. 400, where the painter has failed notably to achieve success. It might be said of many if not of most Cypriot Mycenaean vases with scenic designs that they betray the native Cypriot tendency to overstep the limitations of convention, but these attempts usually end in success and Cypriot figure-scenes are usually better than those on mainland Mycenaean wares. The tendency to emancipation is perceptible on rare occasions also on the mainland : see Wace in *Archaeologia*, Vol. 82, Plate xviii.

[2] *Cesnola Collection*, Nos. 755–9.   *B.M. Cat. Vases*, I, ii, C. 817.

his main forms. The isolated design of a gold brooch or amulet, of which there must have been many in Cyprus, thus led to the isolation of the design on vases. The simple native potter looked no farther than his prototype and reproduced it faithfully or with his own personal elaborations on the side of a small oenochoe. Geometric design is pushed off the main design-surface of the vase, and finally ends as a mere stripe round the base of the stumpy neck. It was in this demand for plain spaces and in the filling of them with only one main theme that the Cypriot artist showed how he was tiring of the dull repetition of Cypriot Geometric styles. These bird-oenochoai can be considered as the first and, in many ways the most attractive of all Cypriot ceramic inventions of the Hellenic Age. But the painters did not always select birds, and even among the varieties of birds depicted there is immense variety. It is a thoroughly live style. One remarkable oenochoe in the Cesnola Collection shows in black silhouette, a ship, apparently of true Hellenic type. Another shows a running man, a third a man-headed bird, less competent in treatment.[1] In this latter, as in others,[2] influences from Assyria seem to have been operative. Once and again the unsubdued Cypriot tendency to a free and emancipated style makes itself evident. One of these oenochoai [3] shows a horseman depicted in a style which might be a survival from the time of the Mycenaean

[1] Nos. 761, 762 and 753.
[2] Myres (*Cesnola Collection*, p. 96) notes an Assyrian or Hittite convention.
[3] *Cesnola Collection*, No. 768.

chariot craters.   The artist has thrown off completely even this relatively new Orientalizing convention and has drawn exactly as he wished.

No fixed dating for this series of bird-vases has yet
been established ; they may be earlier than or contemporary with the splendid 'barrel-oenochoai'
which represent the highest point attained by any
Cypriot pottery and show the full flood of Oriental
influence. Their simplicity suggests that they are
earlier, but on the other hand they may represent
merely a cheaper form of the richer type. Excavation
alone can give the relative dating. I propose here to
take the simple oenochoai and the ' barrel-oenochoai '
as two instances of the same Orientalizing movement
that was sweeping over Cyprus. A good instance of
a link between the two series of vases is seen in a
simple oenochoe in the British Museum [1] where a
design more appropriate to the larger conceptions
of the ' barrel-oenochoai ' is employed. The design
in question shows a chariot drawn by one horse
advancing at the gallop. The driver leans forward
holding the reins while facing backward is an archer
drawing his bow. The heavy semitic cast of countenance of both figures is typically Cypriot, but not
necessarily a proof of Semitic origin. The term
' Greco-Phoenician ' for these vases has long been
abandoned. The faces in this, as in most of the others,
are heavy and semitic because the prototype is certainly
Assyrian. Whether it reached the painter of the vase
direct or through the medium of Phoenician objects
such as the bronze, silver and gold bowls of Phoenician

[1] No. C. 837.

origin so common in Cyprus (see above, p. 132) does
not matter. It is Cypriot work and even in Attica
in the earliest non-Geometric pottery one can often see
the influence of portable Phoenician and other Oriental
works of art. These Cypriot adaptations bear exactly
the same relationship to the Oriental prototype as do
Anglo-Saxon adaptations of the tenth or eleventh
century to the Byzantine prototypes that inspired
them. In this particular oenochoe we see reason to
warn us against hasty assumptions that the simple
globular oenochoai are the earlier of the series. The
more elaborate decoration of this vase is of the type
common to the ' barrel-oenochoai '.

In any case it is in these two varieties that we find
the most fully developed and interesting examples
of the first Cypriot Archaic Orientalizing style. For
once in the history of Hellenic Cyprus of the Iron Age
artists really developed a style which can stand comparison with all but the very finest and best of mainland
Orientalizing styles. It is a style often as good as much
proto-Attic ware, generally more vivid and pictorial
than any Early or Middle Corinthian ware, but rarely
so adept as the better Rhodian vases or the finest proto-
Corinthian. As ceramic it is inferior to anything in
the rest of Greece. For the clay is the usual greenish
coarse clay of Cyprus common in so many periods ;
the paint is so absorbed by the clay as to lose all lustre
and, the shapes, while utilitarian to the highest degree,
are not in themselves beautiful. But their main
interest lies in their richness and in the extraordinary
originality of composition. Nowhere else in Greek
lands, and certainly in no Oriental land, was any kind

of pottery made on which such large and complex designs were used or in which the design had the rich appeal of embroidery. The Orient is interpreted in the light of the coloured and decorative life of Cyprus. As such, these vessels tell us a very great deal about Cypriot reaction to the intrusive Oriental influences.

The larger ' barrel-oenochoai ' are made in a singular fashion. The body of the vessel is turned on the wheel and closed at each end. This egg-shaped body is then placed horizontally and a neck is inserted in the side. The simple globular form of the ' bird-oenochoai ' is thus flattened out and the vessel develops an elongated body. The true front, that is to say, the face of the vessel intended to be seen, is that away from the handle, for there is painted the design, almost always heraldic in form, which is on the vase. The hind-part of the vase is usually unpainted. This deliberate Orientation of the vases is made the more definite by the common practice of giving the facing heraldic design a central axis, usually in the form of a lotus-bud or of a conventionalized plant or tree usually described by cataloguers as a ' sacred tree '. This desire to provide a central axis is not only Greek in character but essentially east Greek or Ionian.

The variety of the designs on these oenochoai is as astonishing as their complexity. The mixture of Oriental elements is as obvious as is the Cypriot nature of their combination. In most cases the ' sacred tree ' or the lotus is the axial controlling element. It is supported sometimes by birds of the type seen on the bird-oenochoai, sometimes, but more rarely, by human figures. The Cesnola Collection contains by far the finest group of this series. The finest of the Cesnola group is undoubtedly that which shows two standing figures wearing a chiton, fringed at the bottom.[1] The figures face outwards, wear bracelets on their arms and act as ' supporters ' in true heraldic fashion to the lotus-tree. The lotus-tree itself sprouts into buds above and below, but in the centre acquires an almost Geometric formalism. This tendency to centralized formalism in the design is almost constant in the whole series. A clue to the character of the standing figure may be found, as Myres points out, in the fact that they wear on their breasts a charm which reappears on some of the sculptured ' temple boys ' found in sanctuaries. They are hieratic figures.

The importance of this particular vase is that it links up Cypriot vase-painting with a type and style of Cypriot sculpture of the sixth century. Throughout I propose to consider these vases as the ceramic equivalent of the Orientalizing process equally evident in sculpture in the Cypro-Archaic period.

Usually the supporters on the designs of these vases are animals. Stags and goats are common. One of the finest known examples is in the Ashmolean Museum. The treatment of these animals suggests some comparison with the goats and stags of Rhodian pottery, but the comparison is one of subject rather than of style, for the Cypriot vases represent the animals in that heavy and more rotund way peculiar to so much Cypriot drawing and always show

[1] No. 751. Illustrated in Myres's catalogue.

a preference for vertical rather than for horizontal attitudes. Rhodian painters show an almost unvaried preference for horizontal attitudes in zones.

The slow development of Cypriot Geometric design into this rich and varied style can best be seen in two shapes, which are far more common than the luxurious and obviously expensive ' barrel-oenochoai '. The kylikes and amphorai exhibit from the earliest Geometric Age down to the late Archaic a constancy of shape which shows how they met a definite and permanent demand among Cypriots. The kylikes in the Geometric Age usually carry a simple panel decoration. The panels are filled with single ornaments such as swastikas or rosettes and divided from each other by groups of vertical lines. A characteristic example is No. 596 in the Cesnola Collection, with closely fitted handles and high stem essentially different from the ordinary Greek kylix. The shape persists and in Nos. 676 and 677 of the same collection is seen a kylix where lotus in one case and bird in another take the place of the panel ornaments. But the panel division still retains the Geometric conventions. In one other respect the Orientalizing kylikes follow the Geometric—they have a double zone of design. In the two instances mentioned the upper zone is purely Geometric, consisting of parallel horizontal lines, but in other instances, such as Nos. C. 814 and 815 in the British Museum, the upper panel shows tendencies to outstep the Geometric. Indeed, No. C. 814 may be taken as a typical example of a Geometric kylix expanding its design into something which is no longer Geometric and not yet Oriental.

Exactly the same process can be seen in the amphorai. Purely Geometric amphorai contain nothing but lozenge and line ornament.[1] This is developed into something more elaborate and elegant as time goes on.[2] Then, while the shape remains unvaried hardly by a hair's breadth, the Geometric ornament gradually develops into an astonishing intricacy and fullness, while on to it are grafted elements of the new Oriental motives. Unexpectedly in a purely Geometric design appear unusual novelties. The conventionalized moth or bee[3] slips into a pattern otherwise rigidly composed of lozenges, squares and hatchings. The lotus multiplies with intense rapidity among these Geometric formalizations. But it appears as a clean intrusion, not as a garbled Geometric version.[4]

Occasionally the amphora develops a style identical with the embroidered style of the 'barrel-oenochoai'. No. C. 853 in the British Museum has a central zone of lotus-trees, below it a zone of lotus-flowers and

[1] E.g. *Cesnola Collection*, No. 501. *B.M. Cat.*, C. 752 and C. 763.

[2] *Cesnola Collection*, No. 608 and a krater, No. 613.

[3] See Payne in *B.S.A.*, XXIX, p. 295. For a fine example of this type see B.M. No. C 851 where the two zones of the base design are derived from proto-Corinthian conventions. Payne's article is of the highest value. It shows the widespread effect of Cypriot Orientalizing art. The 'bee-design' in Cyprus is not originally intended to represent a bee. It is probably derived from an earlier Mycenaean design. But it goes from Cyprus to Crete where it is interpreted as a bee. Much Cypriot influence moulded the Orientalizing ceramic of Crete. Polychromy, the sacred tree, and many elements of Cypriot ceramic went direct to Crete.

[4] See B.M., Nos. C. 841 and C. 849 and *Cesnola Collection*, No. 699.

leaves and above a simpler zone of lotus-flowers, with a further zone of rosettes round the neck. This is one of the most elaborate amphorai of this series.

The style appears fully developed on other shapes such as the stamnos, the feeding-bottle, the aryballos and the pyxis.

The direction from which these Oriental elements came is clear and limited. The Assyrianizing figures and the Hittite character both of figures and of formal design indicate the usual Anatolian and Middle eastern connexions which Cyprus had always maintained. But Egypt contributes more directly. The use of blue paint indicates a direct borrowing, for it is the blue paint common on Egyptian ceramic at all periods, a paint made from calcium-copper silicate [1] and used for the painting of faience as well as ceramic. This blue and the association of reds and browns and occasionally yellows in the matt painting of the 'barrel-oenochoai' adds to the vividness of these delightful vessels. The red is a traditional Bronze Age Cypriot colour. Yellow is a fashion imported from Egypt in the XXVIth Dynasty. Blue comes in a little later. These colours give, in effect, a more striking version of the Orient as interpreted by Greeks than on any other Greek wares. Patterns may lack the grace and elegance of Oriental motives interpreted by other Greeks of the mainland and the islands and Ionia, but they testify to the warmth and intricate love of complex design characteristic of Cypriots who, so long accustomed to Oriental art, yet were always ready to adapt it to their

[1] See Lucas, *Ancient Egyptian Materials*, p. 284 ; Myres, *Cesnola Collection*, p. 92.

own peculiar tastes. The ' barrel-oenochoai ' constitute the most interesting and at the same time the most important artistic contribution of Cypriot vase-painters to the history of ceramic.

Early Cypriot sculpture must be considered as a major manifestation of the same general artistic movement which produced Cypriot ceramic of the type described above. The demand for sculpture appears more or less suddenly and, as the art developed, so it encountered, immediately, precisely the same stimuli that had affected the vase-painters. Whether the stimuli reached the sculptors in the same order or with the same intensity is a matter for which there is no conclusive evidence. But the same regions of the Oriental world served both kinds of artist.

Students of Cypriot sculpture are apt to recoil with alarm when faced by the enormous mass of unimportant, trivial and even hopelessly bad art that confronts them. The quantity of material available is also astonishing and to some extent forbidding. The explanation for the survival of so much Cypriot sculpture is to be found in several causes. One, already referred to, is the ease with which the soft Cypriot limestone could be worked and the abundant quantities of clay available. This made it possible for artists to develop in many parts of the island. There was no city which did not have its local supplies of these materials. The same conditions, however, may be common in other parts of Greece without the same effects ensuing. This is not the sole cause, only a contributory cause. A further contributory cause

was the widespread existence of artistic patronage
which was a necessary consequence of the institution
of kingship, with the royal courts and concentrations
of wealth that would naturally result from such a
political system. But most important of all was the
type and shape of the average Cypriot sanctuary. It
has already been observed that in all Cyprus throughout its period of independence from Greek control
as well as during its subservience to Persia and to
Egypt, no temple of normal Greek Doric, Ionian or
composite type was built. Pending unexpected discoveries it is equally likely that no temple was built
of normal type until Roman times. Even then the
temple at Paphos retained its ancient and peculiar
character and bore no resemblance to any known
building in the ancient world later than the very
end of the Bronze Age. The average Cypriot place
of worship was not a temple of Greek type but rather
an open temenos with minor sacred buildings inside
it and a large number of votive statues freely standing
in the open court, in the manner of dedications on the
Acropolis or at Delphi and Olympia.[1] A typical
sanctuary of this kind, fully excavated, is that at
Idalion.[2] Here there seems to have been a primitive
cult-area that began immediately after the end of the
Bronze Age. This earliest cult-place is considered by
the excavators to have been of a ' very rustic and
primitive type : a sacred enclosure fenced in by twigs,
brushwood or other easily perishable material '. Later
when the Acropolis of Idalion was fortified the cult-

[1] Pryce, B.M. Catalogue of Sculpture, I, ii, p. 5.
[2] S.C.E., Vol. II, Text, p. 627 ff.

place, now inside the walls, consisted of ' an altar court probably enclosed by a hurdle-fence with a square altar of stone as the sacred centre and a cult-chapel of the *liwan* type adjoining the court '. In the late seventh century this temenos was enlarged : the cult-chapel retained its ancient shape but was repaired and a second altar was added of the same type as the first and earlier altar. The temenos was roughly rectangular. The whole sanctuary hardly changed its shape and nature from beginning to end. The deity here worshipped seems to have been Athena, judging from available epigraphical and other evidence, known to Phoenician devotees who also dedicated objects in the sanctuary, as Anaït. These deities were generally regarded in Cyprus as identical,[1] though the Cypriots seem to have worshipped Athena and other goddesses anonymously or simply under the title of Lady of Idalion, or whatever city was in question. As such the goddess was the religious symbol of the independence of the city and, at least at Idalion, the cult ceased when the city was enslaved by its neighbour Kition.

This particular Idalian cult seems in the Bronze Age to have been a fertility cult, like the much more rustic cult at St. Irene, to be discussed below. For on the floor of the cult-room near a small altar were deposits of olives and other vegetables and fruits. Sacrificial waste was placed in *bothroi* outside the cult-houses. Although the temenos changed its character in the Hellenic period and seems to have started afresh, it is most probable that the same fertility rites

[1] Op cit., p. 628.

persisted. While the dedicatory objects found here were mostly of small size and not sculptural, the sanctuary seems to be typical of most Cypriot sanctuaries. In the courtyard were placed the sculptures of devotees.

A similar but smaller sanctuary was found on the north-west coast of Cyprus far from any urban centre, but midway between Soloi and Kyrenia about twenty miles distant from each. It was clearly a shrine for the use of peasants and its discovery puts us in the position of having accessible an unlooted shrine, scientifically excavated, and when found, complete with almost all the dedicatory objects ever placed there. Since the bulk of these objects were terra-cotta statues of great size and importance, and since they were found exactly as they had been left when the sanctuary was abandoned, the value of this particular site to the study of Cypriot sculpture in general and of the art of Cypriot terra-cotta in particular, is obvious. Its excavation does much to atone for the continuous looting of such sites by a previous generation as well as for the unfortunate absence of records of sanctuary sites such as that of Apollo at Voni near Khytroi, or of that of Tremithousa, or that of Aphrodite Kourotrophos at Idalion. The first produced enormous numbers of statues in stone and was excavated for the Cyprus Museum by Ohnefalsch-Richter in 1883, the second was looted by peasants in 1893 and the sculptures so found confiscated, while the third was found ransacked by illicit excavators, with statues left lying on the surface. No doubt there still remain many unexcavated sanctuaries, but at St.

Irene is the only complete and undamaged shrine yet available for strict archaeological study.[1]

This strange and isolated shrine began at the close of the Bronze Age and lasted until about 500 B.C. It thus covers precisely the vital period of Cypriot sculpture and provides full evidence for stylistic development in terra-cotta sculpture in the most controversial period. The Bronze Age sanctuary consisted of a priest's house and store-rooms, as well as a central cult-house. It resembles the Bronze Age sanctuary of Idalion, and was the centre of a fertility cult. Frequent dedications of bulls indicate that in origin it was a fertility cult in which a bull symbolized the fertility so worshipped. After the close of the Bronze Age the early sanctuary was not destroyed but deliberately covered over with earth, and it is probable that the original cult-object, which is thought to be identical with an oval stone in the later temenos, was taken over from the earlier shrine. The stone was the object of actual worship, the bull a symbol of what was in fact adored. For stones are often the cult-objects of fertility cults. The new sanctuary was built over the buried sanctuary of the Bronze Age. An open oval temenos was now built, surrounded by an earthen wall. In the temenos was a low altar and a libation table for fluid offerings. Waste matter from sacrifices was placed, as at Idalion, in *bothroi*. Dedicatory bulls of terra-cotta were placed round the altar. At the close of the Geometric period the temenos was recast, but no new features were introduced : human and Minotaur figures of terra-cotta were now added.

[1] *C.S.E.*, Vol. II, Text, p. 642 ff.

Some are martial in character, indicating that the god was a god both of fertility and of war. From the close of the seventh century further changes and enlargements were made. The same altar is in use, but the temenos now measures some 40 by 30 metres. A rubble and hurdle wall was built around it. In one place a small enclosure for sacred trees seems to have been made. A prodigious number of terra-cotta sculptures, many of life size, were found. They were placed in concentric semicircles round the altar, the smaller figures being nearest the altar and the largest at the back. No inscriptions were found. The statues are evidently dedications commemorating an offering made to the god. They thus differ from actual objects of ownership dedicated, such as scarabs and ornaments, normally in daily use. A severe flood inundated the sanctuary about 500 B.C. and it was thereafter abandoned except when, in the first century B.C., an attempt seems to have been made to revive the cult. This revival hardly lasted more than a century, and from then until its excavation the site remained unknown and forgotten.

The vast group of terra-cottas, crowded round the altar like the mute audience of a theatre, constitutes one of the most amazing discoveries in Cyprus yet made. They seem to be the product of artists of no mean ability and the largest are, technically, works of great skill ; for the art of baking large-scale terra-cotta figures was not one which could be easily learned or practised by mere amateurs. Some school of north-western Cyprus is responsible for the major works of art from the sanctuary.

At this point it is important to decide what the statues in Cypriot sanctuaries were supposed, in the mind of the dedicator, to represent.

Throughout the history of Cypriot sculpture the artist is limited both by demand and by convention. The demand was consistently and almost rigidly for votive statues for dedication only in sanctuaries and the conventions were fixed by those who controlled the sanctuaries—presumably the priests. Thus in Cyprus, failing the evidence from future excavations, we can exclude almost entirely both cult-statues and decorative statues made for public places or streets. Even in Ptolemaic times the bulk of statues seems to have been intended for sanctuaries, and only in Roman times in some few cases does the public statue or the statue designed for a villa or garden, solely for aesthetic purposes, seem to have come into existence. Cypriot art was controlled by its utilitarian purpose almost from beginning to end. In this respect it merely emphasizes tendencies already apparent throughout the Greek world, and often minimized or forgotten. As a general rule, Greek non-architectural sculpture in the sixth, fifth and early fourth centuries was mainly concerned with shrines and sanctuaries and only exhibited itself outside these limits in the shape of tombstones, which need not necessarily be in public cemeteries, and of occasional cult statues of oekist or deity erected outside temples and sacred enclosures.

One of the immediate consequences of the Cypriot sculptor being under the control of the sanctuary was that his statues had to follow two plain rules : [1]

[1] See Pryce in *B.M. Catalogue of Sculpture*, I, ii, p. 5.

A. That they were not to be in the nude, though on occasions the partly nude was allowed.

B. They were to be in full festival dress.

Both these rules were a direct contradiction of the unfettered freedom of the Greek sculptor elsewhere, and they contributed largely towards the development of that dullness and repetitive quality which is the first thing to strike students of Cypriot sculpture in stone or clay.

As to the meaning of the votive sculptures—for, after all, they are no more gratuitous instances of the aesthetic and creative spirit acting independently than any other examples of Greek sculpture—we are in little doubt. They represent neither the deity worshipped nor the dedicator, but rather an ideal, idealized or actual personality which, to the deity, would be the most welcome representative of the dedicator at the sanctuary.[1] The presence among votive statues of a large proportion of identifiable portraits of princes and queens and governors in the Ptolemaic and Roman periods rulers of Cyprus, suggests, as Mr. Pryce hints,[2] that ' the temple enclosure was thus filled with a throng of kings and queens '. Arguing backwards from this suggestion, which the later evidence so strongly supports, it seems most likely that in the sixth century and early fifth we can identify, in some of the splendid regal figures which are typical of this period, certain Egyptian kings such as Amasis and Psamtik III and the great Persian dynasts Darius and

[1] See Pryce in B.M. *Catalogue of Sculpture*, I, ii, p. 5.
[2] Ibid., note 2.

Xerxes.[1] In the earliest types of bearded male such as the superb colossal head acquired by Cesnola [2] now in New York, it may be permissible to see Cambyses. This Persian influence is more evident still in the rare type of turbaned head (B.M. C. 77 and C. 78) which reproduces a type of turban definitely found in Achaemenid portraiture.[3] The fortunate discovery of the complete population of the sanctuary at St. Irene enables us to judge of the preponderance of possibly identifiable regal characters in a limited period preceding the full Classical. Here the bulk of the life-size and colossal terra-cotta statues give the appearance of being portraits of men of power and importance. Some may be actual priests, one in particular wearing a priest's conical cap, priest's Oriental dress and with priest's sacrificial knives in his belt. The rest look as though they were intended for kings and princes. For

[1] Type 16 of the British Museum classification shows a consistent personality or type, bearded, moustached and wreathed, and, if garbed in Hellenic dress, still strongly Persian in appearance. Cf. also *Cesnola Catalogue*, Nos. 1351 and 1352. The former shows a Darius-like figure rendered in the conventions of Greek dress and hair, but with an Oriental cast of countenance and an Oriental pointed helmet. Stylistically it should date to the close of the sixth century and the time of Darius. 1352 is more Oriental in dress but of the same date. No. 1355 is of fifth-century date and might be intended for Xerxes. It belongs to Type 16 of the B.M. classification.

[2] Myres, *Catalogue*, No. 1257. Also cf. No. 1258 and B.M., No. C. 74. The Assyrian conventions of beard and features are what we might expect from a period when any fixed Persian artistic portrait conventions had not yet developed. The dating given by Pryce for this type is about 550, perhaps too early.

[3] See forthcoming *Survey of Persian Art*. A bronze portrait in the collection of Mr. Joseph Brummer at New York.

the most part they seem as local as the style in which they are rendered. They may be intended for priests and kings of Soloi or Marion. These statues from this particular sanctuary form a specific group quite distinct from the large number of statues which may be classified simply as ' ideal votaries ' without any special reference to any actual personality.

This class forms by far the largest class of all Cypriot statues and is the class from which most Cypriot collections in our museums are composed. It is found from the beginning to the end of Cypriot sculpture and was the ordinary dedication of the man of moderate means and ambitions, often perhaps bought ready-made from a sculptor's stock.[1] We can thus with tolerable safety divide Cypriot dedications into two main classes: (1) the simple ideal votary and (2) the specific personality statue. To these two classes a third may be added which ranks third both in quantity and in importance; it consists of statues of deities and legendary figures dedicated irrespective of the deity in whose sanctuary they were put up.[2] A subdivision of this class is that of the Temple Boys, which represent, like the votary statues, servants of the god. But their presence in the temple would be more gratifying to the deity than that of a votary who has no specific task to fulfil.[3]

There were other forms of dedication, some appropriate to a particular shrine, like the Minotaur figures

[1] See Pryce, op. cit., p. 5, Myres, *Cesnola Collection*, p. 128.
[2] It includes figures of Herakles, Zeus, Ammon, Geryon, Artemis and Aphrodite. See *B.M. Cat.*, Types 24, 25 and 26 and 39, 40 and 41. *Coll. Barracco* (a Herakles), Pl. 21.
[3] *Cesnola Collection*, Nos. 1204–1222 and p. 128.

at St. Irene,[1] or of general interest, such as horsemen or chariots.[2]

The origin of the practice of sculpture in Cyprus is an important question that needs the fullest discussion. A priori it is in the highest degree improbable that the art of sculpture would have developed in the island before its development in the rest of the Greek world without the rest of Greece taking from Cypriot sculptors much of their technique and their style. This is patently not the case : indeed, the reverse is evident, for there is no instance of early Cypriot sculpture known which has characteristics which are found only in Cyprus. Cypriot sculpture, early and late, is always derivative, both in essential style and in inessential attributes and detail. While there is always a Κύπριος χαρακτήρ perceptible in every sculpture in the island, it consists not so much of an essential style as of the mode of interpretation of a style invented by some non-Cypriot artist. In the same way the style of painting so immediately recognizable as Flemish is, in fact, a mode of rendering the style of Italian painters, itself authentic and original, current among painters of the Low Countries. So the Cypriot sculptors aimed always at making their own versions of an art invented in other lands. In this the Cypriot sculptor stands apart from Greek sculptors in the rest of the Greek world. Failing the discovery of authentic Cypriot sculpture which owes

[1] *Swedish Cyprus Expedition*, II, p. 785, Pl. 227.
[2] *B.M. Cat.* Type II and *Swedish Cyprus Expedition*, II, p. 789, Pl. 234, 235.

nothing to outside sources it therefore becomes impossible to assume that Cyprus was engaged in the art of sculpture at a date before the rise of sculpture in Attica, the Peloponnese and eastern Greece. So lively was the Greek mind, so prone to adopt inventions made elsewhere and develop them independently, that it is inconceivable that Cyprus would have invented the art, practised it for several generations and left no impress of its invention on the rest of the Greek world.

So much for the *a priori* argument, which has considerable force. When we turn to Cypriot sculpture itself we find nothing in stone or terra-cotta which can be classed as pure invention of the islanders without external stimulus. Indeed, what we do find is a reflection of all the styles of those regions of Greece and of Greek settlements which were in fact nearest to Cyprus. At St. Irene, for instance, which covers the whole Cypro-Archaic period, we can see all the Hellenic styles of eastern Greece, of Naukratis and of the Greek islands, jostling for supremacy.

If we examine the archaic sculpture of Cyprus what we find is a series of works of art which give the appearance of being based on a ' Kleinkunst '. Statues of large or normal life-scale look like enlargements of small terra-cottas, bronzes and stone statuettes brought in by the usual medium of trade. True, this is another *a priori* assumption, but it is susceptible of proof just as is the similar assumption which is usually made and accepted in regard to Anglo-Saxon sculpture and its Byzantine ' Kleinkunst ' prototypes.

The terra-cotta figures which seem to be on grounds of style and fabric the earliest show, as might be expected, a jumble of varied strains of influence. The Cretan loincloth appears both in terra-cotta figures and in stone statues.[1] But the typical Cypriot costume, the leather jerkin, persists for a long period.[2] Itself it may well be a survival of the Mycenaean jerkin.[3] The prevalence of the *mitra*, so popular in Crete, and its persistence down to the end of the sixth century as shown by its occurrence on the full-scale figures from St. Irene, shows some clear contact with the artistic traditions of that island.

But it is more in the structure that the clue to external influence will be found. The earliest type of terra-cotta statuette in the classification at St. Irene, has a trumpet-shaped tubular body.[4] This suggests the influence of the sculpture and terra-cottas of Samos and Miletus.[5] It may be to some extent hazardous to predicate such a connexion on the parallel of body-shapes only, but the fact remains that the trumpet-shaped body is the earliest and that it replaces in popularity a system of making terra-cotta figures, inherited from the Mycenaean and Geometric Age, which was largely amorphous and without any specific body-shape at all. Immediately on the heels of this Ionian strain comes a direct influence from Naukratis. The interconnexion of Naukratis, Samos, Rhodes

[1] Terra-cotta, *S.C.E.*, II, Pl. ccv, 1. Stone, *B.M. Cat.*, C. 7.
[2] *S.C.E.* (at St. Irene) II, Pl. cxci, ccii. *B.M. Cat.*, p. 12, Fig. 1.
[3] Pryce, *B.M. Cat.*, p. 12.   [4] *S.C.E.*, II, Text, p. 786.
[5] Pryce, *B.M. Cat.*, p. 6, n. 2. 'The "snowmen" appear all to be of Ionian extraction and their bell-bottoms recall the Hera of Cheramyes. This would date the Ionian influence to the decade immediately preceding the Egyptian domination under Amasis soon after 560 B.C.'

and Miletus is illustrated both by historical and
artistic evidence.   This Naukratite influence is so clear
as to be beyond dispute.[1] A series of heads and
statuettes show this positive connexion.   Parallel with
it but not, I think, of earlier date [2] is another series
that shows influences from Cretan sculpture.

Whether the influence from Naukratis came in before
or with the Egyptian influence that coincided with the
rule of Amasis over Cyprus is undecided. It was at any
rate possible for both Samos-Miletus and Naukratis to
influence the island in the first half of the sixth century.

The control by Amasis is usually dated to 560–525.
Egypt had looked to Cyprus both for an increased
supply of bronze and for new sources of iron,[3] now
that she had realized, if later than most lands, the
advantages of that metal.   There was also in Cyprus
an unlimited supply of good forest-wood for ship-
building.   The Egyptian fleet of Apries won a victory
in 594 over Cypriot power,[4] but it was Amasis, with
his philhellene interests, who decided to conquer the
island.   Egyptian interests in Cyprus coincided also
with some direct Hellenic contacts, for Solon's visit
to Soloi and Aipeia [5] is dated to the decade immediately
preceding Egyptian control.

Sculpture having developed in the island independ-

[1] *B.M. Cat.*, C. 7, C. 27 and C. 30 and Type 28 and p. 94 (the
female votary).   Merriam *A.J.A.*, 1893, p. 184 ff.

[2] *B.M. Cat.*, C. 1 and C. 3. *Cesnola Collection*, 1251. The
facial shape and the use of rosettes suggests comparison with the
Prinias sculptures.

[3] Myres, *Cesnola Catalogue*, p. xxxvi.   [4] Ibid.

[5] Plutarch, *Solon*, 26.   Aipeia is probably the ancient name of
Vouni.

ently in the generation preceding the Egyptian conquest, the Egyptian artistic influences that now were
predominant, found fertile ground. The main Egyptian statue-type to attain popularity was the Pharoah-
portrait. It gave dedicators an opportunity to display
their loyalty to the new régime as well as to indicate to the deity of the shrine the fact that they
were adorning his precinct with royal figures appropriate to the splendour required. Thus from about
550 Cypriot sculpture is a version, and a far closer
version than Cypriot art was of any other style, of
the pure Egyptian of the Amasis period. The prototype also encouraged work on the colossal scale and
the increased wealth of the island due to Egyptian
exportation of Cypriot raw commodities, led to an
increase in general magnificence of dedication. The
Cypriot adaptations of Egyptian garb and artistic
detail show clearly enough that we are dealing with
Cypriot artists copying Egyptian work but altering
it to suit their own taste. The nude, even above the
waist, is avoided and Egyptian garments like the
shemti [1] are modified to suit Hellenic taste and fashion.
The Egyptian pose is sometimes abandoned and replaced by the Hellenic. True portraiture is of frequent
occurrence and in this respect archaic Cypriots broke
clear from Hellenic custom. With the close of the
period of Egyptian control about 525 B.C. the demand
for Pharaoh-portraits naturally ceased. But Hellenic
influence continued and the normal Greek island nude
kouros-type deeply affected the island sculpture. It had
already made itself manifest in the Naukratite period, but

[1] Pryce, *B.M. Cat. Sculpture*, p. 17.

later it was reinforced by the innumerable *kouroi* which Cypriots could see and study in Samos, Naxos and Miletus. But the influence of these nude *kouroi* was not immediate : it developed more towards the end of the sixth century when Hellenic nationalism rose in strength and the Ionian Revolt was imminent. Nor were the rules of sanctuary-guardians and the innate dislike by Cypriot artists of statues devoid of festival garb likely to promote the popularity of the nude. Like many eastern Greeks, Cypriots seem to have developed little interest in the forms of the human body as such.

When the rise of the new Persian monarchy absorbed both Assyrian power and Phoenician, and had reduced Egypt to impotence, the Cypriots fell into the comprehensive net of the new power. When exactly Cyprus was formally incorporated in the Persian empire is not known. Probably it was taken over during the campaigns of Cambyses, for it is included under the Fifth Satrapy of Darius. Cypriot kings now grow richer and Cypriot life is even better endowed than it was under Amasis. The cities now begin to issue their coinage and, if we can take the case of Vouni palace as typical, local princes embarked on ambitious architectural enterprises. For that the ancient kings of the Cypriot kingdoms existed with much the same power and authority as they had always had, there seems no reasonable doubt.

With the advent of Persian control it might have been expected that Cypriot art absorbed the qualities of Persian art, just as it had absorbed the style and taste of previous masters. But it must be remembered that Persian art as such did not establish a distinctive style until the last quarter of the sixth century and that time would have to be allowed for that newly-forged style to influence the island art. But by the time Persian art, as represented by the very distinctive style of the Achaemenids, had reached a stage when it might have been in a position to influence Cypriot artists, it had already been supplanted by the archaic styles of the Greek islands and mainlands. As we have seen above, the influence of the new masters is manifest in the character of Cypriot sculpture rather than in its style. The dedicatory figures here tentatively identified as Darius-figures and Xerxes-figures, on the analogy of the earlier Amasis-figures and the later portrait-dedications of Demetrius Poliorcetes or the Ptolemies, show that the subject-matter was Persian, but the style overwhelmingly Hellenic. Examples of such sculpture are seen in the head No. C. 76 in the British Museum where the hair and beard are in the pure Hellenic island or mainland style, as is also the rendering of the mouth and ears. Yet a comparison with the head No. 74 in the British Museum shows that, some twenty years earlier, the beard and eyebrows are purely Oriental in style, based on Assyrian work, and the mouth and nose are similarly Oriental, yet the structure of the face, the eyes and facial moulding are not markedly different from those of the later head. This comparison shows how, on a background of native competence which owed its origins to Hellenic contacts, there was added at one period the conventions of a long-established Oriental art and, soon after, those of the Hellenic world. Both heads wear the native Cypriot ear-flap cap which

survives all alien influences and lasts into the fifth
century. The splendid figure in the Cesnola Collection, No. 1351, is one of the masterpieces of this
new Cypro-Hellenic style. Again the Cypriot helmet, similar in type to the leather cap of the preceding
figures, appears ; yet there is nothing in style and garb
about this figure which is not Cypro-Hellenic. The
arrangement of the locks of hair above all, and the
careful cutting of the folds of drapery, all indicate
the direct influence of eastern Greek work. This fine
statue—itself an instance of the real brilliance of this
period of Cypriot art—belongs to the close of the
sixth century. There are many other figures which
can be associated with this to form a coherent group [1]
and it is clear that this period of Cypriot sculpture
was one of the most inspired and fertile.[2] The increasing Hellenic influence coincided with an increased
political sympathy with Greece and Greek international
aims. Consequently when the Ionian revolt began
to take shape, Cyprus, or that part of it which was
most Greek in blood, sided against Persia with the
Greeks. Kition and Amathus, the former by now
the principal settlement of immigrant Phoenicians, the
latter partly Phoenician and largely autochthonous
Cypriot (see above, p. 68) alone stood out against
the revolt. But the Cypriots were soon subdued.
The Phoenicians loyally aided the Persians against the

[1] The St. Irene site gives parallels in terra-cotta : e.g. Nos. 2106,
2103 and 1727 show the same type in a more rustic style : the
statues are life-size.

[2] One of the most delightful creations of Cypriot archaic art is
the turbaned girl-figure, exotic and lovely, one of the most unusual
modes of sculpture in the Greek world. Cf. B.M., C. 272–5.

PLATE XIII

I

OENOCHOE WITH BIRD–DESIGN. ORIENTALIZING PERIOD
(*Nicosia Museum*)

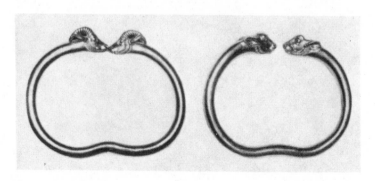

2

ACHAEMENID PERSIAN GOLD ARMLETS FROM VOUNI
(*Nicosia Museum*)

rebellious Cypriots. Kition in the time of Xerxes joined in the siege of Idalion [1] and a state of hostility was in the early fifth century almost continuous between the Phoenician and Cypriot cities. But it was the Hellenic style that persisted, in the sphere of art. Cypriots had openly shown their cultural preferences. The Persian style of art never had a foothold on the island and imported Persian works of art are almost non-existent. The only major Persian works of art extant are the two superb gold armlets found at Vouni by the Swedish excavators.[2] (See Plate XIII, 2.) These can rank among the finest Achaemenid metal-work in existence. One of the armlets has finials worked as wild-goats' heads, the other calves' heads. Both are of the purest style of Persian art of the early fifth century.

Actual imports of Greek works of art in the early fifth century are surprisingly small. The small bronze of two lions attacking a bull, found in the palace of Vouni [3] belongs to the first quarter of the century and is almost certainly an import (Plate XIV). The very fine head, in Greek island marble, in the style of Critios,[4] believed to come from the region of Lapethos, shows that Attic or Attico-Peloponnesian art was appreciated and purchased. An unimportant but well-carved relief in Attic style of the close of the fifth century [5] showing a standing female figure

[1] As recorded in the famous De Luynes bronze tablet inscribed in Cypriot. See Hill, *B.M. Cat. Coins, Cyprus*, p. xxx, and De Luynes, op. cit., Pl. vii, ix.   [2] Not yet published.

[3] Not yet published. Its purpose is obscure. Probably it is an ornament from a tripod.

[4] In the Nicosia Museum. *J.H.S.* 33, p. 48. A Cypriot head inspired by such work is shown in our Plate XV, 1.   [5] Do.

draped in a peplos, indicates that the taste for Attic
work had not declined at a time when Cypriot art
had almost lost its Hellenic inspiration.

The course of Cypriot art after its first enthusiasm
for Greek work at the close of the sixth century is an
interesting study of decline. The highest achievements belong to the period 520–480. Two heads in
the British Museum, Nos. C. 99 and 106 show the
purest Cypriot version of the Hellenic archaic style.
The first is life-scale, with archaic fringe curls surmounted by a typical Cypriot rosette band, an
ornament which adds great beauty to the archaic
simplicity. The second is the major part of a colossal
head with hair and fringe rendered in a convention
which is more a Cypriot adaptation of Greek rather
than anything purely Greek. No marble sculpture
outside Cyprus actually has this convention of hair
and yet in general conception it is based on Greek
conventions. So too, both heads have the eyebrows
carefully incised. But it must be remembered that the
adaptation of Greek island work in marble to the
medium of limestone was bound to be followed by
various technical changes due to the different material
and long employed by Cypriot artists since their first
essays in sculpture.[1] Yet the perfect clarity of design
and execution and the exquisite rendering of eye and

[1] Thus the hollow grooving of the area between the upper
eyelid and the eyebrow, done by abrasion, is a convention which
can be seen in the earliest Cypriot heads. Cf. B.M., Nos. C. 3, 12,
62, 72, 78, and *Coll. Barracco*, No. 70. It is constant through all
foreign influences, Oriental, Egyptian, Phoenician and Greek.
The carefully engraved eyebrow above this groove seems to be
Assyrian in origin. Cf. B.M., C. 74.

PLATE XIV

GREEK BRONZE OF LIONS ATTACKING BULL, FROM THE PALACE OF VOUNI, FIFTH CENTURY, B.C.

(Nicosia Museum)

mouth mark this period of Cypriot sculpture as a great period and suggest that this group of sculptures at this date loses little by comparison with the normal Greek work of the period. A great mass of indifferent work was, it is true, produced at the same time, and Cypriot sculptors rarely rise to any heights of achievement; but enough survives to show that in the island there were many sculptors who can rank high in the history of Greek art.

By 497 B.C. Cypriot rebels had been subdued and the island was once more isolated. To the period 500–470 we may attribute a large proportion of the dull and dedicatory figures, garbed in chiton and himation, which clutter up so many museums.[1] They foreshadow the decline. But there were still masterpieces like the life-size statue in the Cesnola Collection, No. 1355, which must be dated to about 500 or 500–490, or the colossal statue C. 154 in the British Museum which belongs to the period of the Battle of Salamis. Both, as has been suggested, may be Persian monarchs in full Hellenic dress. The influence of the Critios style is evident in many of the votary-figures and its actual presence in the island as a prototype is illustrated by the imported Critian head above referred to. The male statue wreathed in oak, and heavily bearded and moustached is common during the period in question and lasts through to the third quarter of the fifth century. The influence of Pheidias faintly illuminates this period[2] and we see the Hellenic

[1] Type 15 of Mr. Pryce's classification.
[2] B.M., C. 155–6 and *Cesnola Collection*, No. 1291. *Coll. Barracco*, Pl. XX. Cf. Myres's *Cesnola Catalogue*, p. 137. 'The

14

Archaic giving place to developed Attic without the intermediate Olympian style being anywhere evident. Other influences may be detected fleetingly passing over the face of Cypriot sculpture,[1] but none seem to have permanence.

Kimon's exploits at Kition in 449 showed again how Cyprus was under Attic political as well as artistic influence, but with his death it collapses. Nothing now stirs Cypriot art until the nationalist-Hellenic revival under the Evagoras I of Salamis in 410. Cyprus was now virtually independent until it adopted the welcome yoke of Alexander the Great : Persian control during the intervening period had meant little beyond a later restriction of the political power of Evagoras, which in 386 reduced his influence. But his assassination in 374 did not effect the cultural revival he had introduced. The casting off of Persian suzerainty under Alexander was little more than an affirmation of what Evagoras had done.

But the fourth century in Cypriot art is the least known period. It is generally assumed that the decline had become so serious that Cypriot art in this period is no longer worthy of serious attention. Yet two heads (Plates I and XV, 2) from Arsos in the Nicosia Museum [2] testify to an unexpected genius at work, forging a Cypriot conception of mainland work of this age. They seem to be a direct outcome of the artistic revival of Evagoras I. In these two heads one detects

rare examples of Atticized work testify rather to the supreme charm of Attic style momentarily seen and as suddenly appreciated than to any real apprenticeship in this potent school.'

[1] Pryce, op. cit., p. 9.   [2] Unpublished.

PLATE XV

FOURTH-CENTURY HEAD IN LIMESTONE FROM ARSOS

(*Nicosia Museum*)

LIMESTONE HEAD FROM POTAMIA

(*Nicosia Museum*)

hints of what is called 'the Scopasian style' and a suggestion of Praxiteles, but in the main they show us that sculptors were now at work who could adapt the long and rich technical tradition of working limestone into a style which had, outside Cyprus, developed in bronze work and marble. For once the Cypriot technician had his chance and it is impossible to deny that in these two heads, particularly in that shown in Plate I, we see one of the supreme achievements of Cypriot sculpture. The brilliant treatment of the hair and eyes, by which the artist has made the soft stone acquire a quality of strong linear engraving, and the calm beauty of the face and soft surface moulding, give us, for once, a real Cypriot master. There are no other Cypriot heads as fine as this after the Archaic period. The heads seem to be rather the heads of cult images than dedicatory statues. The Demeter of Cnidus suggests comparison, but there is so little trace of direct borrowing in either, that one is driven to presume a local school of real importance whose works have otherwise perished. Their Cypriot origin is, of course, indisputable.

These fourth-century heads stand alone. Further excavations may reveal others of their type and school, but their existence belies the frequently expressed belief that Cypriot art in this century was almost non-existent. Cypriot art has few literary and almost no epigraphical records to illustrate its course. But these heads forbid rash generalizations as to the decadence and decline of the art of sculpture in the island. The finer of the two heads can rank with any fourth-century Greek work extant.

14*

The precision and certainty of touch evident in works of this type is carried over as a tradition into the Hellenistic Age. It is often said [1] that the Cypriot style as such perishes with the Ptolemaic supremacy in Cyprus and the advent of the Hellenistic style and age. It is held also, that the exact opposite occurred and that there was a renaissance of the art of sculpture.[2] What, in fact, seems to have happened was that with the Hellenistic Age Cyprus found itself once more in the limelight and became a wealthier and politically more important place, just as it had been under the first Egyptian domination of Amasis. The result on art was obvious. More dedications were commissioned because there were more rich men to commission them. Almost every sculpture after the advent of Alexander is the portrait of a ruler or his consort. Loyalty, however rapidly diverted to a new objective, seems to have been the mainspring of Cypriot dedicators. This fortunate addiction to hero-worship or flattery (as the case may be) enables us to date Hellenistic Cypriot sculpture with unusual accuracy. Alexander, Demetrius Poliorcetes, five successive Ptolemies and Berenice all appear in the Cypriot national galleries, the sanctuaries. As yet we have no certain information [3] of civic

[1] Myres, *Cesnola Catalogue*, p. 212. ' All trace of Cypriot style has now disappeared ; only the weak provincial handling remains.'

[2] Pryce, op. cit., p. 10. ' The overthrow of the Persian rule by Alexander the Great in 332 leads to what may be termed a rebirth rather than a revival of Cypriot sculpture with new types and sculptors.'

[3] But No. 1902 in the Cesnola Collection is a dedication by the people of Meloucha, the name of which survives to-day in the village name of Melousha.

dedications in public places or of isolated non-religious sculptural enterprises. Our two heads from Arsos find an echo in the fine colossal-scale head of Berenice I,[1] cut in the firm precise style which we see in them. Male portraits have often a similar quality of clarity.[2] The sanctuaries must, indeed, at this time have been richly equipped with colossal portraits which in magnificence outclassed most of the earlier work. The reappearance of the colossal is itself some indication of the increased wealth of the age.

Only with the Roman period can it be said that sculpture in the round finally ceased to be Cypriot. It was wholly Roman and the most notable statue yet found of Roman times is the splendid life-size bronze of Severus, recently discovered at Kythraea.[3]

Relief sculpture stands apart in the history of Cypriot art. There seems to have been little scope for its use, for Cypriots built no temples that required reliefs and never acquired to any large extent the habit of erecting stelai to the dead. But the sarcophagus was in occasional use and provides the bulk of the best Cypriot relief work. No relief of importance or artistic merit precedes the period of archaic Greek influence. Occasional votive reliefs occur, but none of artistic merit. The most striking archaic Cypriot relief is the Herakles-Geryon relief in the Cesnola Collection (No. 1368) where the artist in a negligible

[1] B.M., No. C. 358.
[2] E.g., B.M., Nos. C. 177 (Demetrius) and C. 183 (Ptolemy II), both colossal scale ; C. 191 also colossal.
[3] Unpublished. In Nicosia Museum.

depth of relief has rendered two scenes in two levels. In the upper level Herakles shoots at Geryon's hound, in the lower Eurytion drives away the herds. The purpose of the relief is unknown, but its style clearly shows powerful Egyptian conventions of arrangement, for perspective and for the rendering of the animals. It was probably cut in the time of Amasis and is one of the results of Hellenic Naukratite influence. Its strong Greek qualities differentiate it from much of the sculpture in the round done in the time of Amasis. But it is by no means purely Hellenic in quality. The full Cypro-Hellenic period produces in relief, as in round sculpture, the great masterpieces. The sarcophagus said to come from Golgoi [1] is a splendid work, with reliefs on four sides in a style which owes its existence to the eastern Greek school and the sculptors of Lycia. It is, in the shallowest possible relief, like the Herakles-Geryon relief, and yet it has no elements which are not Anatolian-Hellenic or Cypriot. The lions that surmount its four corners are equally Hellenic. In date it belongs to the time of the Ionian revolt.

Perhaps the greatest of all Cypriot sculptures is the famous Amathus sarcophagus, found by Cesnola, now in New York.[2] A variety of Oriental details and Cypriot elements blend well with a strong Cypro-Hellenic style. It is in high relief. It has been too fully described elsewhere to need further description here, but some of the details deserve attention. The Riders at Arms wear Cypriot helmets, but the horses

---

[1] Myres, *Cesnola Catalogue*, 1364.
[2] That it actually was found at Amathus is now verified. See *S.C.E.*, II, Text, p. 2.

have on their heads the typical Persian feather crest, such as is seen on the Persepolitan reliefs and on the Satrap Sarcophagus at Constantinople.[1] Formal ornament appears as cusp ornamental borders on the rim, with lotus-flowers in formal rows above. Vertical panels show the ' sacred tree ' of the type seen on the vases described on p. 172. The first quarter of the fifth century is the date. It may well be a royal sarcophagus belonging to a King of Amathus. The middle of the fifth century is represented by the recently discovered tomb-reliefs of Pyla [2] where a gorgoneion and flanking sphinxes rendered in separate slabs inserted in the fabric of the tomb, copy with Cypriot limitations, but not unsuccessfully, the mainland and island style of about 460. Parallel with the Pyla sculptures is a fine sphinx tomb-stele in the Cesnola Collection (No. 1413), of a little later. But the sphinxes here are virtually in round sculpture.

A strange and highly provincial stele of Herakles, inscribed in the later Script, comes from Salamiu near Paphos.[3] It also belongs to the mid-fifth century and seems based ultimately on the Greek athletic reliefs of that date like the Nisyros relief.[4] The dedicator is named Aribaos, which is a Macedonian name, and it appears to be dedicated to the cult of Herakles-Horus. The temptation to assign it to the late fourth or third century on this evidence is lessened when we look

[1] G. Mendel, *Cat. des Mus. Imp. Ottomans*, p. 33.
[2] *Cyprus Dept. of Antiq. Annual Report*, 1934, p. 9.
[3] B.M., No. C. 430.
[4] Halil Edhem and M. Schede, *Meisterwerke des Turkischen Museen*, 1928, Pl. vi.

at the style. Presumably a stray Macedonian of the fifth century was the dedicator.

There remains a class of works of art peculiar to Cyprus which must be classified as sculpture. It consists of one-handled jugs, usually without pouring-spouts on the lips, decorated with a separately made plastic figure of a *kore* affixed to the shoulder of the vase opposite the handle. The *kore*-figure in turn holds in her right hand a miniature jug, the base of which is attached to the shoulder of the vessel itself. A channel is made at this point through the shoulder and into the base of the miniature jug, thus making it into the spout of the vessel itself. The wine poured from the vessel thus emerges from the miniature jug.

This whimsical ceramic conception is typical of much that is found in Cypriot ceramic. At all times Cypriot potters indulged in odd inventions and experiments. Multiple vases are common from the Early Bronze Age and quite fantastic shapes are sometimes produced. These *kore*-jugs are a refinement of this tendency. Indeed, they are sometimes of great beauty and elegance. The origin of the type is local. It is to be found in the head-vases of the late seventh and early sixth century.[1]

These head-vases maintain a fairly constant type, with a large projecting spout from the shoulder and the plastic head on the summit of the vase. The shape occurs in various fabrics from developed Geometric to simple red ware decorated with black and purple. They are clearly the prototypes of the *kore*-jugs. The intermediate stage has, however, not been found.

[1] *B.M. Cat. Vases*, No. C. 882 ; *Cesnola Collection*, Nos. 930–5.

The *kore*-jugs appear to begin as a new creation in the period of maximum Hellenic archaic influence. The body of the jugs is usually ovoid and the shape constant. Both the scale and the attitude of the small *kore* remains equally constant.[1] The jugs can be arranged in sequence on purely stylistic grounds, using the *kore* as a test, or else on purely ceramic grounds, using the colour and decoration as a test. In both cases the sequence works out the same. In the *korai* one can see the influence of current Greek mainland and island work over a very long period of time, for the jugs persist as a popular type, quite unchanged, in essentials, from the close of the sixth century down to Roman times. They constitute a quite extraordinary testimony to Cypriot conservatism. As so often in the artistic history of the island, the type of creation is typically Cypriot, the influences that come to bear on it external and alien. Some of the *kore*-figures are of very great charm and they often follow their originals more closely than do many Cypriot stone sculptures. The influences at work are almost entirely Greek. There is hardly a trace of Egyptian, Phoenician or Middle Eastern art in them, and the prevailing Greek influence is, in particular, that of the islands. And in particular among the islands the influence known to us best in the work of Siphnos is predominant, while Samian or Samo-Milesian influences, obvious enough in stone sculpture of the island, are here absent.

[1] Sometimes the *kore* holds the miniature jug with both hands, but usually with her right hand. Variations of attitude rarely go beyond this.

The *kore*-jug is, as far as present knowledge goes, commoner in the west end of the island at Kurion and Marion, but this may be due merely to the hazards of discovery.

The painted decoration of these vases is, in the sixth and early fifth centuries, sometimes of great skill and beauty. It is a black-figure style with incised detail of naturalistic plant forms. The ceramic type, as a whole, is an original and not unsuccessful invention entirely created by Cypriot artists. In detail these plastic vase-*korai* of the archaic type can compare with plastic work in any part of Greece.

Throughout the history of Cypriot sculpture the influences at work that are Greek are all derived from those Greek centres nearest to Cyprus. But the relations with Rhodes are peculiar. There is no trace in the earliest phases of Cypriot sculpture of the Dorian styles of the Peloponnese or of the Creto-Peloponnesian style as a whole. And yet in the island of Rhodes this style flourished with particular vigour.[1] As we have seen, the population of Cyprus was never Dorianized to any appreciable extent and retained its Achaean characteristics down to Ptolemaic times. Probably this Achaean character, which in Classical times, took on itself the nature of Cypriot nationalism, which was reinforced by the substratum of autochthonous Cypriot blood and native Cypriot feeling which expressed itself in the Cypriot script, was hostile to Dorian taste and conventions. The fact remains that Cyprus was invincibly un-Dorian throughout all its artistic history.

[1] R. J. H. Jenkins, *Dedalica*, Pl. xi and *passim*.

PLATE XVI

THE WILD SHEEP (*OVIS OPHION*) PECULIAR
TO CYPRUS

NOTES

To page 39 :

During excavations carried out by the University of Pennsylvania in 1931 at Lapethos, an almost complete vase was found which Professor Myres has definitely identified as a Cretan fabric of the Early Minoan III period. The vase is a two-handled spouted bowl of the skyphos type, comes from Tomb 6. A., and is in the Cyprus Museum.

This is the earliest recorded import into Cyprus and certainly the earliest known instance of Cretan ware in the Levant.

I am indebted to Professor Myres for this information. He examined the vase in question in Cyprus in 1937.

To page 72 :

I have not attempted to discuss the script of the Classical period. Complete tables of signs are to be found both in the British Museum catalogue of coins for *Cyprus* and in Head's *Historia Numorum*. The syllabary is not complete and contains numerous gaps and ambiguities. Only by the aid of a corpus of script inscriptions will it be possible to establish a comparative epigraphy and to isolate local variations. Such a corpus does not yet exist. Inferences back to the Bronze Age script from the Classical are therefore precarious. This book is too small to include any reconsideration of the Classical script, which deserves a volume in itself. I have contented myself with an endeavour to deal with the pre-Classical script only.

INDEX

DATE DUE